Conte

C000192721

Volume 95:4 Winter 2005/6

Poems

Language Says

5	Antonella Anedda	A
6	Amir Or	Language Says
		A Correction
8	Peter Porter	An Absolutist Chorale
9	W.N.Herbert	Catalan
		Tissue Remains
11	Simon Armitage	The Patent
13	Dilawar Karadaghi	An Afternoon at Snowfall
18	Inna Lisnianskaya	*from:* Forty Days
20	Elaine Feinstein	Widow's Necklace
		Another Anniversary
22	Pia Tafdrup	Domain
		Knowledge
24	Kate Bingham	Crying
25	Dennis O'Driscoll	There Was
28	Robin Robertson	Mar-Hawk
		The Glair
30	Gerrit Achterberg	Protein
		Cherubim
32	Arjen Duinker	The Bluebird
40	David Morley	A Boy Casting Snow on Winter Barley
41	Georges Rodenbach	Sundays
43	Neil Curry	Falling Asleep with Henry James
44	Andrew Elliott	These Lines
45	Helen Farish	Posting
46	Herbert Lomas	Le Petit Pont de Pierre

A Musical Interlude

47	Tamara Fulcher	Choirsinger
49	Mario Petrucci	Trombone
50	Chris Preddle	Black
51	Tony Roberts	After the Celibacy of Summer
52	E.A.Markham	Scarves and Benches

53	Sarah Corbett	Rivers, Roads
54	Sarah Maguire	Almost the Equinox
56	Estill Pollock	Transitions of Plane in the Appearance of Attic Korai
58	Michael Ossei	We Love the Lads

Centrefold

61	John Berger	*I Would Softly Tell My Love*
70	John Kinsella	*Line Breaks and Back-Drafts: Not a Defence of a Poem*
79	John Berger	*That Have Not Been Asked: Ten Dispatches About Endurance in Face of Walls*

Reviews

87	Peter Mcdonald on J.H.Prynne
89	David Kennedy on elegy in: Mallarmé translated by Patrick McGuinness, Daniel Weissbort on Brodsky and collections by Esther Morgan and Alan Ross
93	Jan Montefiore on Anne Stevenson, Sheenagh Pugh and Rita Ann Higgins
97	*Feature Review: Prose by Three Women Poets* Michelene Wandor on literary biography by Elaine Feinstein, Ruth Padel's travel memoir and fiction from Bernadine Evaristo
99	*One That Got Away*: Andrew Duncan reassesses John Hartley Williams's latest collection
102	David Morley on John Heath-Stubbs and W.S. Graham
105	Robyn Bolam on Pascale Petit, Sarah Wardle, Jane Yeh and Polukhina & Weissbort's anthology of contemporary Russian women poets
108	Will Stone on Inna Lisnianskaya and on Michael Hofmann's anthology of Twentieth Century German Poems

Endpapers

115	Tõnu Õnnepalu	*Midsummer: Postcards from Estonia*
118	Letters to the Editor	
119	...and a surprise response	
121	*PR Jukebox*	
123	Editorial	
124	The Geoffrey Dearmer Prize	
125	Contributors	
127	Chris McCabe	Coda
129	John Kinsella	Articulated Coda

POEMS

Beyond language, language is a wound
from which the world flows and flows.
—Amir Or

Antonella Anedda
A

is the letter of awe, the vowel that opens the throat. The ah of
breath and relief. Heraldic, thus. A bar across a tower, a triangle on
an empty plinth.

Worshipping (images)
the beauty of tiny gardens and forests,
a chair propped against a wall and vapour from the beech trees.
Looking up at the terrace at the flap of a tablecloth, which for a
moment seems to spread over my heart, soothing it, swelling it
with sky-blue.

*

Abandoning, being abandoned.
Suddenly, after a night in which love is no longer a blessing, in
which the dream has described our bodies on its vault. But the
shapes are lost one by one blowing away the past; first all things in
the great vast sweep of the stars.
Out there, beyond sleep, desire rolls stronger than life.
What we abandon, what abandons us.

Opening the window
to look at the fir tree in all its splendour,
listening to the sound of needles
pouring through the morning air.

Translated by Sarah Arvio

Amir Or
Language Says

Language says: before language
stands a language. Language is traces
stained by over there.
Language says: listen now.
You listen: here was
           echo.

Take silence and try to be silent.
Take the words and try to speak:
beyond language, language is a wound
from which the world flows and flows.
Language says: is, is not, is,
is not. Language says: I.
Language says: come on, let's speak you,
handle you; come on, say
you've said –

A Correction

for the sin of being spoiled with words and mistaking the call of Love;
for turning away from myself like shadow from body, face from heart;
for the sin of 'What will they say?'; for self denial; for pride;
for the sin of having followed the spell of praise under the stage lights;
for my ear that has abandoned listening,
for the utterance of the mouth which I have spoken, yet my soul has not;
for sin I've committed against my own body with the rod and no
                              kindness, beating my breast;

for calling Yours my own;
for having sinned before You by anxiety and vain fear,
for having fed the fire of doubt from the log of the tree of plenty;
for having been dilatory in growing;
for having shut my door and having neither heard nor seen nor let
                              happiness enter me

when beholding Your being.

Translated with the poet

Peter Porter
An Absolutist Chorale

Our God is here, a practical recruitment,
The millions he has killed he cannot see.
He is the Sorry One, the swarm precipitant,
And his an executioner's privacy.

To be alone is every person's gift,
Though crying in the night is a reminder
That Happy Valleys are Depression's Rift.
Confession looks best in a sombre binder.

And these, the very neatest hymns, are made
Not for the Faithful or the purloined critics
But just to show that rebels can't evade
The Ethics, the plump Aristotelian hiccups.

The world should get much better – yes, it should.
It tries, it surely does. What interposes
We're never sure of. Facing what is good
We smell the blood: we cannot smell the roses.

W. N. Herbert
Catalan

It's like a language that you used to speak
quite fluently, but then you moved away
from the household of her hips, and as the weeks
rephrased as years you couldn't understand,
the patois of that profile and those hands
began to slip until you couldn't read
her in the phrases of those other throats
who conjugated you in warmer beds.
You realized that you no longer dreamt
in the sharp vowels of her breast and hair;
the names of her mind's streets had all turned gray
and you could only speak a dialect
which let you say you loved her all the more
though in the wrong case, and the perfect tense.

Tissue Remains

Too many hands were pressing on
my breastbone and my brow in
the great marble sandwich of the state museum.
We slid like sliced meat about the Thracian room
filled with so much gold as though
Midas had beaten up a rose garden
into this dinner service full of slurring *rhyta*.
The bas-relief horsemen insisted
on cornering their boars with always
one hand flung out behind them
not clutching a spear but letting the reins stream
through their casually tugging long fingers
which would only take a millennium
to rearrange themselves into
the next door icons' serpentine blessing machines
of still more hands. But for now
all the faces were Alexander clones
so that was never where my eyes could rest
till the skull-bulb helmets drew us,
their tight-lipped spaces that hold
exact absences, to the case in which
earth-coloured armour propped on perspex shoulders
and shinbones. And the greaves,
that word that's almost a wound,
had their own card that told us
what survives the centuries' ceaseless fingers
is less than the step I couldn't take away:
'Bronze, traces of leather straps, tissue remains.'

Simon Armitage
The Patent

i.m. Michael Donaghy

Last night in the shed he was working late,
perfecting light,

inventing the light-bulb that lasts and lasts.
He believes in lamps

which as well as giving an instant shine
will illuminate over and over again

and, far from being dim, the prototypes
are surprisingly bright

and functional too, being fused
for domestic use.

But the light-bulb people are up in arms.
They haven't come this far

to be put in the shade, outshone
by a light whose licence they claim to own,

by a lamp they invented themselves,
then shelved.

So they're hitting back with a cunning device
which works in reverse,

which soaks up colours
and light until darkness occurs.

Known as Obscurity Bulbs
these dense, inky blobs

are available in a range of marques
from *Evening Murk*

to *Endless Midnight of Fathomless Depth.*
They're very left

field, almost like art,
and the trade-magazines are pushing them hard.

Which leads us straight
to a city, a town, a blotted-out street

whose residents blink
at the clues in the crossword, squint at the book

they're trying to read.
Although... in a garden shed across the road

there's a glint. A man works late
perfecting light,

his hand cupped like some secretive priest
of the ancient past

protecting a flame in the night.
His face in a bulb of glass, like an astronaut.

Dilawar Karadaghi

Kurdish poet Dilawar Karadaghi was born in 1963 and studied Drama in the Institute of Fine Arts in Baghdad. He has published four collections of poetry and a book length poem in collaboration with Nazand Begokhani. He now lives in Sweden.

An Afternoon at Snowfall

I'm not here.
What a shame, tomorrow day will break
and I won't be here anymore.
Shame, I won't be here tomorrow
when someone opens the window,
when someone writes a name
on the window's mist,
when someone waters the flower pots
and, with an intense gaze,
observes the confusion of fallen sparrows.

I'm not here.
What a shame, I won't be here tomorrow
when someone,
still drenched in a blue dream,
slowly staggers towards the mirror,
runs the tap,
and tells the lonely man in the mirror –
a man who has turned to mist,
to a grain of sand,
to a drop of dew –
You silly thing, what a strange dream I had about you!
I swear, you came into my dreams
more than a hundred times last night.

I'm not here.
What a shame, I won't be here
when, in the light snowfall one morning,
his heart racing,
somebody suddenly starts worrying without reason,
wishing that someone,
someone who no longer walks the streets,
someone who no longer walks out the door,
or stares out the window,
will walk past
and say:
I haven't seen you for ages, my friend!

I'm not here.
Shame, I won't be here tomorrow
when someone in a fast train
passes by a small brooding cloud
above a mournful station
and, having a sudden premonition,
calls to the cloud,
raises his hand,
turning round to look back
as it vanishes out of sight,
muttering under his breath:
Maybe that's him?
Maybe that's the one who doesn't exist,
someone who can't ever stop
at a single station anywhere.

I'm not here.
Shame, I won't be here
when in a drizzly hour one morning
in a library –
a library dressed in a tarboush
and a suit,
a library stuffed full of musty books –
a sad poem, sitting in
its own attic of solitude –
a poem which still gazes expectantly

and speaks as clear as a mirror –
is picked up by someone,
the kindest person in the world,
who takes it by the hand
and helps it off the shelf.
Together they leave for
a teahouse near the library
where they sit in the sun
and laugh in the rain,
and putting their hands in their pockets
they whistle in the snow.
As the world passes by
they think about life, considering
all the things that are important
all the things that are simple
and new.
They consider the things
that have been fenced off,
that have been disappeared
and pushed to one side.
They consider a poem
that has not come to life.
They consider an infant
wrapped up in a blanket patterned with butterflies.
They consider an orange seller.
They consider a kite threaded to childhood.
They consider their morning sweet tea.
They consider a blade of grass.
They consider a baby sparrow
risking its first flight through the rain.
They consider a crushed can
tinkling downstream at siesta-time.

I'm not here.
Shame, I won't be here
when a door is opened
but no one walks through.
When a window is open
but no pollen-down drifts in with the evening.

When a ladder dies from waiting
for someone to climb it
carrying a bunch of grapes
up to the roof on a warm summer night.
When a road pines away from loneliness
and no one gives it a hug.
When a tree collapses
and no one remembers its colours.
When a garden is overgrown
and its flowers are never worn anymore.

I'm not here.
Shame, I won't be here
when you come out to the courtyard one evening
and it isn't me
whose finger presses the doorbell,
waiting by the door
with a heart full of doubt like green grapes.

I'm not here.
Shame, I won't be here
when in a cold hour one winter afternoon
you walk out all worried
and it won't be me
who stares like a child at the rising wind
and the falling rain.

I'm not here.
Shame, I won't be here
when one afternoon at snowfall
you walk through the city looking for me.
You search for me in the armpit of a bat.
You knock on the door of an ant friend of mine;
worried, you ask, Haven't you seen him today?

You stop a drunk squirrel's truck.
You enter an owl's flower shop.
You coo along with a pessimistic pigeon.
You stop by a garden related to me
to look through the closed fists of flowers.
You search through the straw under the house of a stork,
in the beaks of fledgling sparrows,
in the claws of a hedgehog.
You look through the depths of a drop of water for me,
you search under a ladybird's feet,
beneath a crumb of clay,
inside the warm heart of a stalk of wheat,
in the bitterness of a haw,
under a bruised leaf of basil,
beneath the tongue of a speechless *zikzike*,
in the corner of a dank pocket of a story,
in the iris of a bead,
in the sleeve of a rhubarb stalk,
on the roof of a fresh smell,
in the middle of a bundle of dreams,
under the skin of a snowflake,
in the heartbeat of a pomegranate seed –
in everything.
You will search for me in everything.
What a shame that at that sad hour of the afternoon
you'll be looking for me
but I won't be here,
what a shame that
on this afternoon as snow falls
I'm
not
here
anymore.

Translated by Choman Hardi and the Poetry Translation Centre workshop

Inna Lisnianskaya
from: Forty Days

30 April 2003

I let the last hour go of your life,
And your blue eyes

Glazed, staring at the skies.
How absurd it all is!

For thirty days, you've shunned my dreams –
You'll not pardon me

For noticing, in this light of hell,
How, over the trees, the clouds

Had parted, letting you through
To join all the rest in paradise.

30 April 2003

I bathed your eyelids, chest, belly
With water from the tap
And pressed the open wound of my mouth
To your cold lips.

I stifled my widow's cries,
A pillar of salt am I,
Positioned by your bedside
This late spring time.

Only the Lord sees,
Only an angel keeps watch.
For strangers my day is ordinary;
Your life, too, was such.

1 May 2003

Unsteady, like a writing-stand,
I write to you by the light of the stars,
Where the birds are building
Their unearthly nests. And ours,

Made of wood, with its little porch
Where you'd sit on the steps,
Is encircled by Saturn's ring
And diminutive triangles

Of birds that made themselves nests
In our pine-needly yard. At dawn
They share, as far as they can,
A widow's grief with their minute of silence.

Translated by Daniel Weissbort

Elaine Feinstein
Widow's Necklace

Friends try my stories on their teeth or
with a match: are they plastic or amber?

My children say I must have forgotten
how I used to turn to them so very often,

repeating your words and begging reassurance.
Why should I now recall a loving presence?

But so I do: my story as a wife
is threaded on the string of my own life,

and when I touch these beads, I still remember
your warm back as we slept like spoons together.

Another Anniversary

Today is your birthday. There is cool sunshine.
Fig leaves and roses cover the wooden fence.
What happiness can I wish you in your death?

Here is the garden that I made for us
though you saw only the winter shape
of a weeping crab apple and a bare plum.

It was my offering. And so you received it.
Yet most of what we work at disappears.
Little we worry over has importance.

The greedy and the generous have the same end.
The dead know nothing and we cannot speak with them.
Still, in that silence, let me write: *dear friend.*

Pia Tafdrup
Domain

Suddenly – as milk boils over
                   in a lonely house
where no one is ready to take the pot off the flame,
suddenly – between what is past
and what is to pass,
when a star lights up the day,
the memory of the crematorium's smoke
ascending from the chimney –
dimly twisted fossils
             of naked pillars.
A wave rises,
       light rushes up from the earth.
My sister and I wear sunglasses,
because we mustn't be seen
as the blind wheels of the hearses roll by,
but would like to say farewell...
The grown-ups give the children salt
when they are thirsty,
only the earth is wet with dew
and the shadow
beneath flowing white flowers cools the day.

Knowledge

In the light of the soul's dream the chestnut leaves are hammered
by the sun to gold,
the tree throws them off, but the pigeons in the elm tree
have made a mistake and have young ones now,
and you
are a tower of happiness and threatening expectation.
You light the strongly scented leaf,
raise me in a spiral with your gaze.
The sun behind driving rain clouds,
the sun in a semi-circle around us,
from window to window, dizzy
as the blood murmurs in the finest capillaries:
The silence sings,
but we don't suffer from fear of heights,
we climb stiffly,
crowned by crows' cawing,
balance and climb further in the gale
which is mild as a springtime, as hands and lips,
but comes towards us in gust after gust,
while all around collapses –
falls
to the earth, where the wet darkness grows
in yawning chaotic formations...
We shall possibly lose one another from sight again,
but like the intense colours
the blind man sees in his sleep,
the skin wants to remember where it was touched
by zigzag of flying hands, by roaming lips,
by a tongue that suddenly travels
to places surprisingly authentic and obscure,
as though it wanted to know the end before the beginning.

Translated by David McDuff

Kate Bingham
Crying

They cry because they're babies, babies cry –
they're hungry, uncomfortable, need to sleep
or sometimes for no reason you or I

however anxiously we empathise
can guess, or for no reason but to keep
us guessing night and day, they cry and cry.

They stand up, learn to walk and talk and tie
their shoelaces. You watch them cross the street
without holding hands, but sometimes I

fall over at school, half-strangled, as they fight
for one more last goodbye; and let them weep
when I am not at liberty to cry.

Their swollen soft distracted faces dry.
Mine is forgotten. Free to drag my feet
unsupervised back through the playground, I

will be late for work, but sometimes stop to spy
on them, or in a flash of childish pique
call out their names, want them to see me cry,
their fat transparent tears escape my eyes.

Dennis O'Driscoll
There Was

there was a house
woodsmoke was part of it
drinking water rinsed in peat
trace elements of cloves and sage
December light was in it
grey as a collared dove

spontaneous gatherings
of rainwater
were funnelled down
the gullies of the sloping lane

above the hooked cooking utensils
on the open hearth
the kitchen chimney made
a look-out post from which
you monitored the sky
that sad-eyed creature
outdoors in all weathers
brushed with mushy cloud

there was a moment
it had a waftage of frankincense
logs came from a toppled trunk
your uncle dragged bodily
from the hilltop forest
like the antlered stag
its mounted head still flaunted in the hall
opposite the mildewed mirror
that tarnished everyone alike

antler leaves defended holly beads
the fuchsia bush beside the roughcast wall
had stood the test of eternity

in the forest where your barefoot
father's school carved out
a limestone eyrie among the trees
laid-back cuckoos
made their eggs at home
each summer robbing nests
my god talk about wildflowers mosses fungi ferns
rustlings from undergrowth stirrings from burrows
tracks and pawmarks badger setts fox scents unlikely birds

you gasped a little at whatever
it was you had within your grasp
clutched it as best you could
sensed its closeness as you passed
the rosewood cabinet from which
an old embossed edition
of *A Christmas Carol* had been removed

brothers sister two girl cousins
played with board-games crayons
winds whining outside
answered to a different world
and the mud-clobbered yard
was revealed only to make
the timbered parlour floor
even more secure under your feet
its heat more precious

unthinkable that your parents
would ever need to retrace
the drab miles home
that your uncle might step
out into that faltering day
with hay or mangels for the cattle

and something in the moment
was brighter for the darkness
warmer for the storm putting pressure
on the rowan tree in the rushy field
more reliable for the tiny squared-off
window-panes in which the scene
was compressed into eye-sized segments

the latch rattles in the flagstoned kitchen
a whispered mist of smoke is picked up
a disturbed log sleeping on the job
buds suddenly into orange-squash coloured flames

a dusk chorus of voices
none is at cross purposes for once
you know from the tone
everyone is in complete agreement
the details can be thrashed out later
meanwhile tea and lemonade are poured
iced tar-black slices passed around

you are clinging
to the candlelit moment
holding its trusted hand
tightly as a flame
attaches to a wick

shake the day
it might start snowing
like the glass globe you agitate –
a blocked salt cellar –
letting loose its grains
on the stable that could
easily be the rattling zinc-roofed
cattleshed outside

snow lodging
within reach of there
can never melt

Robin Robertson
Mar-Hawk

Fed so long on washed meat and tirings
he is sharp-set, but fret-marked: hood-shy
and mantling; he bates at the perch,
won't come to the glove.

When we slip him on sprung quarry
he takes stand in the trees,
or rings up, towering, and rakes away,
unmade, unmanned.

The Glair

The slow drag across the sandpaper,
scratching smoke
from the head of the match
again and again until it flares.
Lamplight lies heavy on her breasts,
her flanks; the hand's passage
slow as ceremony, persistent
as a dream unsleeved; the spark
drawn in hard with a catch
of flame: the lumbering storm
and the white bolt, the bright rope, on
and on and on. The albumen. The glair.

Gerrit Achterberg

Gerrit Achterberg (1905–1962) is a Dutch poet whose first collection Afvaart *(1931) announced his single Orphic theme: to bring the beloved from death to life through the power of the word. After a tragic incident in 1937 in which his land-lady was shot and killed, Achterberg was incarcerated in several asylums until 1945 and was under psychiatric treatment by state order till 1955. In 1959 he was awarded the prestigious Constantijn Huygens prize for his complete literary oeuvre.*

Protein

Eighteen amino acids made
the albumen where you began,
so says the lexicon.
I stare out through the window-pane.

Counting is part of making you come clean
and the millions swarm around
out of your total number –
years and a sum, broken asunder.

Growth-rings draw their tokens out
on the inside parts of dust.
And statistics work their facts.

Measurement and possibility
compose death-testing unity.
I chart the graph of your track.

Cherubim

Slim cherubim,
too early for a name,
without a sex,

you call to the angel,
who waylays you;

who rests in my thighs,
almost a man,
almost expired.

(First round-about...
a dealing-out, so fate would put
me in this body, locked-up...)

And he has risen
with wings, quite conscious
of their time and opening.

He flies back with you
out of my death and into my origin,
where I know you, o cherubim.

Translated by Antoinette Fawcett

Arjen Duinker
The Bluebird

Listen

There is a bluebird

        Listen look

Great sure bluebird

        Sure there is a bluebird

Great sure bluebird

        In history

No waterfalls around

        Bluebird in history

        Because of no mountains around
                  the bluebird

History without mountains
Listen to history

        Without waterfalls the bluebird

On every battlefield in the distance

        Incredible distance
        Incredible bluebird

Red

        Black

Singing on southern shores

        Red

Black

        Singing on northern shores

The bluebird is great
Great and wonderful
Great and incredible

        Around no waterfalls

No waterfalls around
Time in the distance

        Distance in a dream

Dream in the bluebird

Dream in the mouth

Telling jokes to the bluebird

On every battlefield

About great chilies

About great ridiculous chilies

About great ridiculous fantastic chilies

Bonus

Time

Listen

Because time is a bonus

Because the bluebird is different from the distance

Flying in a dream

The bluebird
The bluebird

The bluebird is different
The bluebird is different

Great

Great

Because the bluebird is not a parrot

No train
No bicycle

No other bird

Identity sings twilight
Twilight no train no bicycle

The bluebird like the bluebird no twilight
No identity

The bluebird next to the bluebird

Because the bluebird is not dreaming
Because the bluebird is not a parrot
Because the bluebird is not the same

From the distance

From the distance

In a train

From the distance

In a train with children and tonsils

From the distance

In a train with women and hips

From the distance

In a train with men and claws

Around no waterfalls

Thanks to hips
Thanks to claws

Claws and clouds

Dry clouds

Thanks to hips

Sweet clouds
Dry

Dry the bluebird is great

Nose

Nose cheek nose

Doing lucid things

Dry the bluebird is great yes

In dry clouds doing lucid things

Listen
Marines

Doing lucid things in dry clouds

Loving the bluebird

The bluebird

Loving the bluebird

Dogwood
Hawthorn

Katydids

Katydids loving the bluebird

Dry clouds
Dry clouds

Graveyard

Train with tonsils
Incredible

Incredible marines loving the bluebird

Train
Tonsils

Incredible
Dry clouds dry clouds

Dry clouds dry shadows

Of roses

Kissing a raindrop in naked embrace

Sweet clouds

Sweet shadows

Kissing a raindrop in naked embrace

Roses are red
Roses are black

Moon pushing train

With no waterfalls around

Moon pushing train

Slowly because of time
Slowly because of time

Red time black time

Moon

The bluebird sings

Moon

From the distance

From the future distance
Because the moon is possible

Because the moon is possible

Yes the bluebird sings
On southern shores

In the north
No mountains

Mountains are busy
Yes the bluebird sings

Because the moon is possible

Mountains are busy
Slowly because of time

Flags don't prove any future

Any future any time

Flags and mountains are busy

Flags and mountains are busy

Flags and mountains are busy
Yes the bluebird sings

From the distance

In the distance
Into the distance

Look sweet and dry

Dry clouds

Dry clouds dry moon

The bluebird

Table

Off the record

Through red windows

Through black windows

Off the record

Sure bluebird

About tickets and time

Mountains busy throughout history
With tickets and time

The bluebird

Time

Truth and time are not the same

Truth and time are not the same

Look

Look sweet and dry

Look clouds and moon

Table

Chair

The bluebird sings dry clouds dry moon

In a room in a chair

The bluebird sings red windows

In a chair in a room

Yes the bluebird sings truth

Yes the bluebird sure sings truth
Tickets
Time

Throughout history

Buying history

The bluebird
Tickets

Throughout history

Throughout history

Dogwood

Red
Black

Yes red black

Truth and time are not the same

Hawthorn

Incredible look katydids incredible

The bluebird is great

The bluebird is great

Great incredible red black
Great incredible red black

Great incredible red blue
Great incredible black blue

Seaweed

Seaweed
To sing in bottles
Seaweed

To place a bet in cans

The bluebird after determination
The bluebird after determination

Seaweed sure bluebird

Hawthorn katydids

Yes red black

Yes red black

Dogwood

Katydids

Nose cheek nose

The bluebird is great

The bluebird is great

Determined to sing

Shores full of seaweed

Seaweed determined to sing

To place a bet in bottles

Cans and caravans singing
Cans and cases singing

Through windows

To place a bet in bottles

Seaweed sure bluebird

To sing without history

To sing without waterfalls

Red black

To sing without
Sure bluebird sure

Next to a secret

Blood
No table

The bluebird

Next to a secret

The bluebird is expecting a secret

Expecting a secret
Expecting a secret

Because the moon is possible
Because the bluebird is expecting a secret

Hips possible claws

Despite blood despite voices
Despite blood despite the comb

From the distance

To sing determination in history

With no waterfalls around

To sing listen katydids

To sing look katydids

A secret

A secret bluebird incredible
Incredible seaweed

No chair

The bluebird beautiful blood

Because the bluebird

The bluebird beautiful blood

In bottles and cans
Off the record

The moon is possible

A train leaving hips possible claws

Thanks to the comb
Thanks to voices

While the bluebird is great and incredible

Dry clouds cruel grammar

No words without cruel grammar

Incredible with no waterfalls around

The bluebird is great and incredible

Singing dry clouds dancing dry clouds

The bluebird

The bluebird

The bluebird radiant

The comb of the radiant bluebird

Sure and radiant
Radiant and incredible

Incredible and wonderful comb

Because of a blanket
The radiant bluebird

A blanket of lashes

The bluebird drops the comb
On a blanket of lashes

The bluebird drops the comb
On a blanket of lashes

David Morley
A Boy Casting Snow on Winter Barley

A variation of Celan

The months are hairs combed over each other, or crushed
papers in a cellar. December is growing, fur on my lip.

December's the hair on a monk's fingers, a book pulled open,
a boy throwing snow at the first winter crops. Your hair is twisted up;

it is dark and it makes me imagine shells or cloud-shells, a boat
nudging into a rainy lake. A boat, a book pulled open or over,

fear, a shrew squirming in my fingers... December's black hook.
December's lake water. Can I sing? Can I live through this winter?

A small lyric on my palm. I stand on the shore of a lake.
As far as a boat may be rowed, the colour of aspens

colourless by night as I grow in shade and my age deepens.
I speak of loving you as I speak to you about hands,

shells or clouds. I push the boats with my fingers and they nod
in our bloodstreams, lovers crushed together, or clouds

heaped in a downpour. Walking from the forest I find myself
necklaced with bared hands. December is gaining on me.

Georges Rodenbach

Georges Rodenbach was born in Belgium in 1855, grew up in Ghent and spent much of his adult life in Paris. He is chiefly associated with Bruges, location for his most celebrated and influential work, the poetic novel Bruges-la-Morte *(1892). He also wrote a number of collections of poetry, of which* Le Règne du silence *(1891) in many ways prefigures* Bruges-la-Morte; *a further more complex novel* Le Carilloneur *(1897), also set in Bruges; several books of short stories; prose poems; and a range of essays. He died aged 43 and occupies a distinctive tomb in Père Lachaise cemetery.*

Sundays

Mournful Sunday afternoons in winter,
in the drowsiness of provincial towns,
where some inconsolable weather cock

like a bird of iron, creaks alone on a roof-top!

And drifting on the wind who knows what anguish.
Rare passers-by travel the pavements:
priests, working women in great black hooded cloaks,
beguines returning from the parish service.

The faces of listless women are pressed
to the pane, gazing on the void and silence,
and a few meagre flowers, settled in somnolence,
achieve their death in the veiled frames.

And in the space between the curtains
in drawing rooms of large patrician mansions
one might see, on backgrounds of old gobelin tapestry
in ancient frames of gold, ancestral portraits,

in velvet doublet and ruffs of lace,
coats of arms at each corner of the canvas,
who as a star is lit scan the far distance
and the town sleeps on in heavy silences.

And all those old mansions are empty, lifeless;
within them, seeking refuge, the dead middle ages;
and so it is, at evening, the luminous sun
seeks refuge too in their melancholy lanterns.

Oh lanterns, guarding the memory of fire,
the memories of light long disappeared,
so dejected in the affliction and emptiness of the street
they seem to burn for the cortège of some deity!

And now of a sudden the restless bells
disturb the belfry planted in its pride,
and their sound, heavily bronzed, gradually falls
on the coffin of the town as if in spadefuls.

Translated by Will Stone

Neil Curry
Falling Asleep With Henry James

The wrongly placed (as it had seemed to him)
Apostrophe got up upon its several
Tiny feet, strode purposefully across

The margin, and began a traverse
Of the ridges of his index fingernail.
In the meantime, Miles had passed his arm

Around his little sister and was reading
To her as they walked together, up and down,
In the garden. No doubt an English

Garden with flowerbeds – nothing to match
The Villa Rincón and its high cool terraces,
The grey-green leaves of the olive trees

Set off by the wrinkling blue of the sea.
Page fifty-six was where his marker was.
The children had evidently gone inside.

But not the pair of ladies, who were deep
In agitated conversation. Fifty-eight.
The cicadas had stopped, leaving behind

One of those silent moments when the world
Seems to have gathered itself together
And be crouching. The younger of the ladies

Was threatening to leave. A pine cone dropped,
And he had the uneasy feeling there was
Someone else looking out from underneath

His eyelids and leaning their elbows
(Could it be Quint?) on the sills of his skull.
And in that instant nothing seemed to him

More natural than that these things, as he
Had read somewhere, should be those other things
Which clearly they were absolutely not.

Andrew Elliott
These Lines

Try, please, to imagine this line like a red flag unfurling
And underneath it, black, a line of people marching
Through snow so deep, so white this line would be invisible
If not for the line, the last, its task to hold up everything.

Helen Farish
Posting

Sometimes I think about his posting
to HMS Affray, how it was changed
at the last minute, someone in authority saying
R A Farish (like picking a name from a hat),
R A Farish you will live, you will be posted
to another submarine, to one which will not sink
drowning all on board, carrying their lives,
their future wives, their children, their joys and woes
into the tide that did just what tides do.

You will live, R A Farish, another 40 years free
from headline catastrophes but not free
from those small print catastrophes which take lives
cell by cell in the small unspoken print of life.
I understand now how woe wrote itself
cell by cell, how it took you breath by breath
night by night to that moment
in the doctor's surgery, someone in authority saying:
R A Farish, here is the hat, here is your name.

Herbert Lomas
Le Petit Pont de Pierre

The little bridge's ochre stones
obliterate their weight with their own tensions.

Their ochre's the wild ochre of the bushes,
but they're more taught than the bushes,

as if self-aware of their rakish arc's
acrobatic airwalking precariousness.

With no handrail and the raving blue ravine below
none but the unvertiginous will dare the stones.

How lovely to die in that blueness,
if dying weren't such a large question mark.

A Musical Interlude

Tamara Fulcher
Choirsinger

My father said, So what do you do?
I stopped, and replied, I sing in the choir.

Choir? said Mother, That must take some work.
I said, It takes a lot,

And practice. He flicked his ash
Into the hearth and I tried to stand taller.
It fell as small snow. My shoes were tight.
Do you perform?
Not on my own, Ma, I said, But we do.
Who?
The choir. We are many. She dropped her head
As he made a noise.
Outside was getting in, between the drapes.

I wish you'd told us, she said,
We'd like to have known before now.
The fire cracked. He made the noise again,
Looking down.
We could have come to watch.
You can still come, I said, eager as a boy.

Oh, I don't know. He could still speak
To throw me off. He sucked on the end of it,
Chucked it in to burn. It's a bit late for that now.
Season's nearly over, eh.
There is no season, I said. There is no season,
Mother said, pushing in,
It's all the time. He rubbed his red hands fast.
Oh well, he said, You'll let us know how

You're getting along.
What do you sing? she said, craning up.
Oh, I said, Just songs. Everything.
Yes, we said, Yes. He was still looking
Down at the wood, white, shaking into air
And fading out of sight, out of being.
I saw her eyes were closed.

Mario Petrucci
Trombone

I saw this guy once
work his cylinders so

hard the pistoned brass
seemed to drive some

massive axle only he
could see – grinding at

that same good yard of
track – his stalled truck

-load of jazz getting no-
where sliding on grease

yet charging up on itself –
charging till all our stacks

were leaning forward weak
with smoke: flagging for that

held-back stroke when
finally he'd give it

sand

and notes (taking sudden
grip) would fling us

steaming with him out and
into tunnels down

glinting girdered rails
of sound

Steam locomotives carried sand to drop on the rails when traction was lacking.

Chris Preddle
Black

The quartet lift their fiddlebows
like eyebrows, and pause. Dressed in matt black,
four just men, they commence their labours

with Haydn and Mozart, then ply the baleful Bartok
with its high anxieties. As we leave
I think, as if more were needed! We're late back

at Holme, where the moors with one resolve
sit down like black cattle hearing thunder in the index.
I must fetch in coal, and dig with a tiny shovel

into the bunker. The coals, manufactured hexa-
hedrons and ellipsoids of revolution,
revolve and roll away like disaffected eggs

that I dropped as a child in a film-noir version
of an egg-and-spoon race. They will not cohere,
the blackguards. On Black Hill the television

transmitter mast we can see from here
sticks up like a lifted bow. The quartet pause, with elbows
poised; there's something I still need to hear.

Tony Roberts
After the Celibacy of Summer

After the celibacy of summer,
The last movement of Haydn's 'Farewell'
Has freed each instrument in turn,
And now they are making off

Across the lawns of the Esterházy palace,
One at a swallow-tailed time:
The wanton oboes and the horns,
Engorged bassoons, priapic strings,
The carnal bass drum *con abbandono*.

They leave in their wake
The dry old Kapellmeister,
Strewn strawberries, crushed canapés,
A clatter of upturned chairs,
A smatter of surprised applause
As the fat-arsed cello
Crashes an ornamental pond.

Meanwhile the wives of Eisenstadt
Pay scant attention to their prayers.
One turns a mattress, another a curl.
With heightened colour and tapping feet
They shuck their silks and soak themselves.
Tonight it will be chamber music.

E.A. Markham
Scarves and Benches

Scarves and benches come together only at those times
when the mind taking a rest without your noticing
is jolted out of it and cautions you to pay heed.
That's why on losing my scarf I think of Horace, a mad fellow
to those who didn't know him: for what do you say of a man
without means erecting monuments to a relative
who thought him mad? First there was a bench on the island,
then other benches in places where the sitters would be foreign.

Scarves and benches come together now that I've left another
valued strip of silk on some bus or pavement indifferent
to the vanity that once sought it out and thought its splash of colour
a small trick to put upon a grown-up day. I liked the benches
for their wooden life, random and not designed to be immortal.
Not sky-threatening, close to the ground as if in tune
with a man from a small island, or of small stature, a man
in casual mourning for a world that, surely, no one made.

I deny that this shedding of silk at random will serve to link
one journey with another in any special way. Though it hurts a little
to be anonymous once again; and the chance collector,
proud of this find that won't defend its shape as if it mattered,
is your invention. So scarves and benches come together as when
your sentence not written down won't be recalled, and shufflings
of the grammar all refuse to fit. So what can I say? Scarves
are less permanent than benches. Scarves are a good form of litter.

Sarah Corbett
Rivers, Roads

Rivers are roads, cutting their borders.
Roads are rivers, sutures on muted greens.
Small spots are signs, circles on hills
or gradients on a frozen tarn depth rings.

Wave tips telescope; there are engine rainbows.
The end of land has been expertly carved.
Wings are joyful above snowfall cumulous
in the blue clear beneath the cirrus.

Pools are erasures, the creeping cars creeping,
white diagrams of houses paths for worship.
A wooded copse is a crop of hairs
repeated like dropped aitches in the hollows.

Beauty is elicit, and the city just left
a milk-caul, frost on leaf, just that.

Sarah Maguire
Almost the Equinox

and the Thames so emptied of current
it shows bare flanks of sand. Beige sand. A beach.
The sudden vertigo of hardness when we're cupped
over the walls of the Embankment

examining the strange cream stones below,
driftwood, bottle-tops, crockery, one sodden boot.
And the slow mud opens its mouth.
Jets long departed, their con-trails fire

across the fierce blue skies, unfurling
into breath. The very last weather of a summer
spent impatient for change,
waiting for a sign, an alignment.

Beneath our feet, a hemisphere away,
the full moon tugs fluids into tides, and stops
another night in its tracks,
hours before it climbs over London –

the constant pull of elsewhere
mooring us outside ourselves. The colchicums
come naked into the early autumn air.
Bruised into mauve and purple,

their frail blooms admit the memory of harm
in their risky flight to beauty. Packed bulbs
underground harbour their secrets.
Now that we have witnessed

the flare of that ginkgo spilling up
besides St Paul's – its roots woven
deep beneath a graveyard of graves,
its slim knotted branches, sleeved

with airy, fantail leaves –
it will come back to us, suddenly,
years from now. Anomalous Jurassic relic,
its origins are as ancient as these slabs

of blackening Whin-bed Portland Stone,
set here by Wren to stamp out Fire and Plague.
As a child, I climbed all the stairs
to the Whispering Gallery, laid my cheek

against the painted plaster of the dome,
and let those perfected acoustics bear my changed voice
back to myself. The huge nave
reminds you of the Great Mosque in Kabul –

sunlight falling on pillars of stone, the hushed intentness
of prayer. Shattered, war-torn, it's still standing,
somehow, next to the river by the Bridge of Bricks,
just as Wren's great dome once soared above the Blitz,

intact. Tonight, we will look up to see
Mars, that old harbinger of war, come so close to us
it rivets the southern sky with its furious,
amber flare. Sixty-thousand years ago it lit

these heavens and looked down
on ice. Next convergence, nothing will be left of us
leaning on this bridge of wires and tempered steel,
wondering at the river and the city and the stars,

here, on the last hot night before this planet tilts us
into darkness, our cold season underground.
The tide has turned, the Thames comes inching back,
drowning everything it will reveal again.

for Yama Yari

Estill Pollock
Transitions of Plane in the Appearance of Attic Korai

Beyond the window, in the fields the flax yellows.
Who has taken the months, the festivals,
the deep belly of our flame?
In our memory images of heavy wrong whirling –
slogans and the wreath of blood at the door
with all we owned – a weave of restlessness
and cobwebs, from the missed heartbeat finding
no way back.

Rain soaks the fires. We are condemned
by seconds sinking silently in space.
The sun hangs on the ropes of morning. It is itself,
as high as the day, the stories disintegrating
along the way we went,
the place without reason never reached,
with everyone singing through dust
and black loaves and the names of slaves
a salt burn in the mouth.

Tyrant shadows enshrine the sun.
A thousand times blacker, the lunatic
unrolls the parchments out of memory, out of hope,
droplets of music marking the hour,
the scaffold, the crown, the henchman's axe, the burst of blood
a red lark in compasses of poplar leaves.

We are walking in rain, silver linden, meadows the dead
came to, my sisters as tall as flowers.
In the old battlefields
Antigone
the pine sap clings to birdsong – flowing through us.

The world is deceived, not smelling the blood, the deeper sun
captive in plain scarves of cobwebs and terror,
this meaning of bread and flooding light,
a prayer to gods older than burials,
in the oat and through the catacomb
where the well springs and the stink of the dead
is washed from us,
in the first fall of the first sun, in the yellow dew of torchlight,
carrying our own ashes, the high silver of the stars
we climb to.

Michael Ossei
We Love the Lads

I saw Stan Mortensen sitting
on the rim of one of those long
toilets and pissing endlessly
on the floor. When I came in, he

called me a nigger. I told him
to fuck off and die because he
was a has-been (we'd just beat the
infamous 1780

forward line of Finney, Matthews
Mortensen, Lofthouse etc
at five-a-side). Then I went and
complained to a white teacher and

friend about Mortensen's conduct
and they were sympathetic. I
moaned that they didn't really know
how these things hurt and they were still

sympathetic.

CENTREFOLD

It's how we are taught, maybe choose, to read that matters.
—John Kinsella

I Would Softly Tell My Love

JOHN BERGER

Friday

Nazim, I'm in mourning and I want to share it with you, as you shared so many hopes and so many mournings with us.

> The telegram came at night,
>   only three syllables:
> 'He is dead'.

I'm mourning my friend Juan Muñoz, a wonderful artist who died yesterday on a beach in Spain, aged 48.

I want to ask you about something which puzzles me. After a natural death, as distinct from victimisation, killing or dying from hunger, there is first the shock, unless the person has been ailing for a long while, then there is the monstrous sense of loss, particularly when the person is young –

> The day is breaking
> but my room
> is composed of a long night.

– and there follows the pain, which says of itself that it will never end. Yet with this pain there comes, surreptitiously, something else which approaches a joke but is not one (Juan was a good joker), something which hallucinates, a little similar to the gesture of a conjuror's handkerchief after a trick, a kind of lightness, totally opposed to what one is feeling. You recognise what I mean? Is this lightness a frivolity or a new instruction?

Five minutes after my asking you this, I received a fax from my son Yves, with some lines he had just written for Juan:

> You always appeared
>   with a laugh
> and a new trick.

> You always disappeared
>   leaving your hands
> on our table.

> You disappeared
> > leaving your cards
> in our hands.
>
> You will re-appear
> > with a new laugh
> which will be a trick.

Saturday

I'm not sure whether I ever saw Nazim Hikmet. I would swear to it that I did, but I can't find the circumstantial evidence. I believe it was in London in 1954. Four years after he had been released from prison, nine years before his death. He was speaking at a political meeting held in Red Lion Square, London. He said a few words and then he read some poems. Some in English, others in Turkish. His voice was strong, calm, highly personal and very musical. But it did not seem to come from his throat – or not from his throat at that moment. It was as though he had a radio in his breast, which he switched on and off with one of his large, slightly trembling, hands. I'm describing it badly because his presence and sincerity were very obvious. In one of his long poems he describes six people in Turkey listening in the early 1940s to a symphony by Shostakovich on the radio. Three of the six people are (like him) in prison. The broadcast is live; the symphony is being played at that same moment in Moscow, several thousand kilometres away. Hearing him read his poems in Red Lion Square, I had the impression that the words he was saying were also coming from the other side of the world. Not because they were difficult to understand (they were not), nor because they were blurred or weary (they were full of the capacity of endurance), but because they were being said to somehow triumph over distances and to transcend endless separations. The here of all his poems is elsewhere.

> In Prague a cart –
> > a one-horse wagon –
> passes the Old Jewish Cemetery.
> The cart is full of longing for another city,
> > I am the driver.

Even when he was sitting on the platform before he got up to speak, you could see he was an unusually large and tall man. It was not for nothing that he was nick-named "The tree with blue eyes". When he did stand up, you had the impression he was also very light, so light that he risked to become airborne.

Perhaps I never did see him, for it would seem unlikely that, at a meeting organised in London by the international Peace Movement, Hikmet would have been tethered to the platform by several guy ropes so that he should remain earth-bound. Yet that is my clear memory. His words after he pronounced them rose into the sky – it was a meeting outdoors – and his body made as if to follow the words he had written, as they drifted higher and higher above the Square and above the sparks of the one-time trams which had been suppressed three or four years before along Theobald's Road.

> You're a mountain village
> in Anatolia,
> you're my city,
> most beautiful and most unhappy.
> You're a cry for help – I mean, you're my country;
> the footsteps running towards you are mine.

Monday morning

Nearly all the contemporary poets who have counted most for me during my long life I have read in translation, seldom in their original language. I think it would have been impossible for anyone to say this before the twentieth century. Arguments about poetry being or not being translatable went on for centuries – but they were chamber arguments like chamber music. During the twentieth century most of the chambers were reduced to rubble. New means of communication, global politics, imperialisms, world markets, etc. threw millions of people together and took millions of people apart in an indiscriminate and quite unprecedented way. And as a result the expectations of poetry changed; more and more the best poetry counted on readers who were further and further away.

> Our poems
> like milestones
> must line the road.

During the twentieth century, many naked lines of poetry were strung between different continents, between forsaken villages and distant capitals. You all know it, all of you, Hikmet, Brecht, Vallejo, Attila Jósef, Adonis, Juan Gelman...

Monday afternoon

When I first read some poems by Nazim Hikmet I was in my late teens. They were published in an obscure international literary review in London, under the aegis of the British Communist Party. I was a regular reader. The Party line on poetry was crap, but the poems and stories published were often inspiring.

By that time Meyerhold had already been executed in Moscow. If I think particularly now of Meyerhold, it is because Hikmet admired him, and was much influenced by him when he first visited Moscow in the early '20s:

> I owe very much to the theatre of Meyerhold. In 1925 I was back in Turkey and I organised the first Workers' Theatre in one of the industrial districts of Istanbul. Working in this theatre as director and writer, I felt that it was Meyerhold who had opened to us new possibilities of working for and with the audience.

After 1937, those new possibilities had cost Meyerhold his life, but in London readers of the *Review* did not yet know this. What struck me about Hikmet's poems when I first discovered them was their space; they contained more space than any poetry I had until then read. They didn't describe space; they came through it, they crossed mountains. They were also about action. They related doubts, solitude, bereavement, sadness, but these feelings followed actions rather than being a substitute for action. Space and actions go together. Their antithesis is prison, and it was in Turkish prisons that Hikmet, as a political prisoner, wrote half his life's work.

Wednesday

Nazim, I want to describe to you the table on which I'm writing. A white metal garden table, such as one might come across today in the grounds of a *yali* on the Bosphorus. This one is on the covered verandah of a small house in a southeast Paris suburb. This house was built in 1938, one of many houses built here at that time for artisans, tradesmen, skilled workers. In 1938 you were in prison. A watch was hanging on a nail above your bed. In the ward above yours three bandits in chains were awaiting their death sentence.

There are always too many papers on this table. Each morning the first thing I do, whilst sipping coffee, is to try to put them back into order. To the right of me there is a plant in a pot which I know you would like. It has very dark leaves. Their undersurface is the colour of damsons; on top the light has stained them dark brown. The leaves are grouped in threes, as if they were night butterflies – and they are the same size as butterflies – feeding from the same flower. The plant's own flowers are very small, pink and as innocent as the voices of kids learning a song in a Primary School. It's a kind of giant clover. This particular one came from Poland where the plant's name is *Koniczyna*. It was given to me by the mother of a friend who grew it in her garden near the Ukrainian border. She has striking blue eyes and can't stop touching her plants as she walks through the garden or moves around her house, just as some grandmothers can't stop touching their young grand-children's heads.

> My love my rose,
> my journey across the Polish plain has begun:
> I'm a small boy, happy and amazed,
> a small boy
> looking at his first picture book
>   of people
>   animals
>   object, plants.

In story-telling everything depends upon what follows what. And the truest order is seldom obvious. Trial and error. Often many times. This is why a pair of scissors and a reel of Scotch tape are also on the table. The tape is not fitted into one of those gadgets which makes it easy to tear off a length. I have to cut the tape with the scissors. What is hard is finding where the tape ends on the roll, and then unrolling it. I search impatiently, irritably, with my finger nails. Consequently, when once I do find the end, I stick it on to the edge of the table, and I let the tape unroll until it touches the floor, then I leave it hanging there.

At times I walk out of the verandah into the adjoining room where I chat or eat or read a newspaper. A few days ago, I was sitting in this room and something caught my eye because it was moving. A minute cascade of twinkling water was falling, rippling, towards the verandah floor near the legs of my empty chair in front of the table. Streams in the Alps begin with no more than a trickle like this.

A reel of scotch tape stirred by a draught from a window is sometimes enough to move mountains.

Thursday evening
Ten years ago I was standing in front of a building in Istanbul near the Haydar-Pacha Station, where suspects were interrogated by the police. Political prisoners were held and cross-examined, sometimes for weeks, on the top floor. Hikmet was cross-examined there in 1938.

The building was not planned as a jail but as a massive administrative fortress. It appears indestructible and is built of bricks and silence. Prisons, constructed as such, have a sinister, but often also a nervous, make-shift air about them. For example, the prison in Bursa where Hikmet spent ten years was nick-named "the stone aeroplane", because of its irregular lay-out. The staid fortress I was looking at by the station in Istanbul had by contrast the confidence and tranquility of a monument to silence.

Whoever is inside here and whatever happens inside here – the building announced in measured tones – will be forgotten, removed from the record, buried in a crevice between Europe and Asia.

It was then that I understood something about his poetry's unique and inevitable strategy: it had to continually overreach its own confinement! Prisoners everywhere have always dreamt of the Great Escape, but Hikmet's poetry did not. His poetry, before it began, placed the prison as a small dot on the map of the world.

> The most beautiful sea
>   hasn't been crossed yet.
> The most beautiful child
>   hasn't grown up yet.
> Our most beautiful days
>   we haven't seen yet.
> And the most beautiful words I wanted to tell you
>   I haven't said yet.
>
> They've taken us prisoner
> they've locked us up:
>   me inside the walls,
>   you outside.
> But that's nothing.
>   The worst
> is when people – knowingly or not –
> carry prison inside themselves...
> Most people have been forced to do this,
>
> honest, hard-working good people
> who deserve to be loved as much as I love you.

His poetry, like a geometry compass, traced circles, sometimes intimate, sometimes wide and global, with only its sharp point inserted in the prison cell.

Friday morning

It was Juan Muñoz whom I was waiting for in the Hotel Ritz in Madrid, and he was late because, as he explained, when he was working hard at night he was like a mechanic under a car, and he forgot about time. After the Ritz incident he sent me a fax, which I'll quote. I'm not sure why. Maybe the why isn't my business. I'm simply acting as a postman between two dead men.

> I would like to introduce myself to you – I am a Spanish mechanic (cars only, not motorcycles) who spends most of his time lying on his back underneath an engine looking for it! But – and this is the important issue – I make the occasional art work. Not that I am an artist. No. But I would like to stop this nonsense of crawling in and under greasy cars, and become the Keith Richard of the art world. And if this is not possible to work like the priests, half an hour only, and with wine.
>
> I'm writing to you because two friends (one in Porto and one in Rotterdam) want to invite you and me to the basement of the Boyman's Car Museum and to other cellars (hopefully more alcoholic) in the old town of Porto.
>
> They also mentioned something about landscape which I did not understand. Landscape! I think maybe, it was something about driving and looking around, or looking around whilst driving around...
>
> Sorry Sir, another client just came in. Whoa! A Triumph Spitfire!

I hear his laughter, echoing in the studio where he is alone with his silent figures.

Friday evening

Sometimes it seems to me that many of the greatest poems of the twentieth century – written by women as well as men – may be the most fraternal ever written. If so this has nothing to do with political slogans. It applies to Rilke who was apolitical, to Borges who was a reactionary, and to Hikmet who was a life-long communist. Our century was one of unprecedented massacres, yet the future it imagined (and sometimes fought for) proposed fraternity. Very few earlier centuries made such a proposal.

> These men, Dino,
> who hold tattered shreds of light:

where are they going
in this gloom, Dino?
You, me too:
we are with them, Dino.
We too Dino
have glimpsed the blue sky.

Saturday

Maybe, Nazim, I'm not seeing you this time either. Yet I would swear to it
that I am. You are sitting across the table from me on the verandah. Have you
ever noticed how the shape of a head often suggests the mode of thinking
which habitually goes on inside it? There are heads which relentlessly
indicate speed of calculation. Others which reveal the determined pursuit of
old ideas. Many these days betray the incomprehension of continuous loss.
Your head – its size and your screwed up blue eyes – suggest to me the
coexistence of many worlds with different skies, one within another, inside it
not intimidating, calm, but used to overcrowding.

I want to ask you about the period we're living today. Much of what you
believed was happening in history, or believed should happen, has turned
out to be illusory. Socialism, as you imagined it, is being built nowhere.
Corporate capitalism advances unimpeded – although increasingly
contested and the twin World Trade Towers have been blown up. The
overcrowded world grows poorer every year. Where is the blue sky today that
you saw with Dino?

Yes, those hopes, you reply, are in tatters, yet what does this really
change? Justice is still a one-word prayer, as Ziggy Marley sings in your time
now. The whole of history is about hopes being sustained, lost, renewed. And
with new hopes come new theories. But for the overcrowded, for those who
have little or nothing except, sometimes, courage and love, hope works
differently. Hope is then something to bite on, to put between the teeth.
Don't forget this. Be realist. With hope between the teeth comes the strength
to carry on even when fatigue never lets up, comes the strength, when
necessary, to choose not to shout at the wrong moment, comes the strength
above all not to howl. A person with hope between her or his teeth is a
brother or sister who commands respect. Those without hope in the real
world are condemned to be alone. The best they can offer is only pity. And
whether these hopes between the teeth are fresh or tattered makes little
difference when it comes to surviving the nights and imagining a new day.
Do you have any coffee?

I'll make some.

I leave the verandah. When I come back from the kitchen with two cups

– and the coffee is Turkish – you have left. On the table, very near where the scotch tape is stuck, there is a book, open at a poem you wrote in 1962:

If I was a plane tree – I would rest in its shade
if I was a book
I would read, without being bored, on sleepless night,
       pencil I would not want to be, even between my own fingers,
if I was door
       I would open for the good and shut for the wicked
if I was window, a wide open window, without curtains
I would bring the city into my room
if I was a word
       I would call out for the beautiful, the just, the true
if I was word
       I would softly tell my love.

℘

Line Breaks and Back-Draft:
Not a Defence of a Poem

JOHN KINSELLA

For me, the measure of a poem is the word, not the line. This is a re-lineation and slight editing (one line) of a poem published originally (1999) in John Tranter's web journal, *Jacket*:

And Everyone Gathered In Objection Yet Again
for Robert Adamson

And suddenly there was a presence,
as if it were worth something,
the pylons sticking up out of the water
like busted bones out of flesh.

A waterbird landed
but didn't make much of an impression –
a damp squib by comparison –
though a couple of fishermen

couldn't take their eyes off it.
Bloody voyeurs, somebody muttered,
and the bird, as if taking offence,
lifted and vanished

into the confident glow of the poem,
the crowd encrypting itself
into the scene's diffident colouration,
troughed and crested

like the hum of the current.

As written above, it basically subscribes to the one-unit-of-thought-per-line, "natural" if elided clusters of speech, and hypotactic clause structure. The lines, if not end-stopped, are weighted as points of sub-closure within the greater sentence structure of the poem. If the content is not conventional, the layout certainly is, with minor digressions. In terms of what's being "said", the poem is expectedly periphrastic – it's a roundabout journey to get to the main point because there are many other possible points of departure in meaning and tone on the way. However, the predictable lineation limits the possibilities of this periphrasis, unless as readers we read against the line breaks – say, taking random points within an ensuing line as an end/beginning to the unit of (de-)lineation.

Within the figurative expectations of the poem, I performed this "adjustment" in response to a discussion on the poem on a metrics chat site, recently brought to my attention. When I draft a poem with line breaks that go against expected or formulaic (in poetry) speech patterns or, as the commentator on the chat site remarked, "syntactical or rhetorical boundaries", it often begins in that staccato and stilted fashion of much lineated metrical verse. It's a set of ideas and images measured by line breaks – I gain a sense of balance and perspective in the draft, but rarely get the poem as I've seen it in my mind's eye (I literally see poems written before I "copy" them).

In a sense, I back-draft. The original drafts are often comparatively closer to the linguistically controlled specimens that a more formalist poet or reader might desire. Sometimes I let them stay that way if it suits my broader purpose. But through a process of drafting de-lineation, often in fact relying on the physical measurement of a line in a particular font (which often changes when the poem is published) by way of "weighting", using the centre of the line not so much as caesura but as pivot, I distract or displace the expected measurements.

Of course, for me, "syntactical and rhetorical" boundaries are prisons. My poetry is a direct result of my politics and ethics, and form for me is a box to be pushed against; to be used pragmatically at times, but ultimately to be tested at every opportunity. I do not want my poems to give pleasure, I don't want them to be comfortable, and I don't want them to "tell". I want my poems to suggest and to bother – to irritate, and to instigate.

Language for me is a generator, and has an organicism that leads to the myriad creation of meaning (out of context); and so is form. Form is not simply the safe house of aesthetic and artistic control that allows us to know a text is a poem; form is not necessarily the guide to interpretation and instruction many hope for. It's how we are taught, maybe choose, to read, that matters. I don't want to package a poem.

Even in the re-draft, the "dangling" last line might somehow partially gain this effect – a resistance to the bracketings of the previous four-line stanzas – but equally it might provide a more restrictive packaging through suggesting total closure. I see this draft as more anatomically correct than I find enticing. I don't want my poems to leisure or pleasure, but I do want them to allow for a polymorphously perverse interaction with both myself and the reader. They are fetishes, but hopefully with adjustable appendages. They will change with time and place.

The poem cited is not one of my personal favourites. It was written in response to Robert Adamson's great poem of collation and sublimated dialogue with voices of romantic and modernist urges in poetry, 'The Rumour'. It arose from the occasion of a boat ride on the Hawkesbury with Adamson, remembered a few years later in the context of re-reading 'The Rumour'. It's a poem about displacing displaced and re-represented voices. "Packaging" it would be inappropriate. Here's what Adamson had to say about 'The Rumour' in an interview I conducted with him in the mid-'90s – what's crucial in terms of discussing the lineation of my response is that 'The Rumour' was always a poem about process, about a broader imaginary conversation on process and inspiration:

> RA: ...And then I said that to Creeley, "Ah, I understand, I understand," and he was laughing. He said, "Okay, okay that's fine to understand it. I'm glad I can help. But now what you've got to do is write your poem in Australian." I said, "What are you talking about?" I had versions of poems, and that would have been early versions of 'The Rumour', especially that one I wrote before 'The Rumour'. Because it's a bit like Hart Crane, 'The Rumour'. I started it at the beginning and the end, and then filled in the middle. So one of the first things I wrote was that section called 'Everybody Gathered in Objection'. That was an early version. I showed it to Creeley and he said, "Okay, what you've got to do now is write like Ted Berrigan, only you're Australian so..." He looked at a lot of poetry in my house and he couldn't find anything that sounded Australian. I grabbed Bruce Dawe and Bruce Beaver and he said, "Yeah, they're getting there, they're getting there as far as using the language". He said, "I hear this language, I've never known it before but I hear it in the air, I've heard it for three days and I can hear the tune you're all playing."
>
> That's the way he put it. He actually said to me take the high art and put in the language of your everyday conversation. "You're talking to me in poems that are much better than the poems you've got down here on the page." It sounds so simple, it really does, but he taught me how to write down the rhythms of conversation and couple that with – this is just

technical but it wasn't just technical – couple that with the language of high literature or high modernism, whatever you like, and play that off against it. So what will happen then in the technical exercises, you'll find – this is Creeley saying to me – you'll find that steeped in language like that, your subject will arise out of the language. You won't have to worry about where you're taking it, it'll come out, or you know, it's just that when you find the right form you'll have the content. So you know, the thing about that was that, in a strange weird way, Berrigan came into that poem, although there's no traces of it in there.

JK: There's a rumour of it.

RA: Yeah.

JK: A fact, something we know, a scientific fact for example, can be bent, can be altered to a certain end, can be propaganda-ised if you like. A rumour inevitably will be because it can't be reconstructed as fact. How does that notion fit in with the definitive poetics that you're trying to explore?

RA: In the book it's very important, that quote from Wallace Stevens at the beginning, "In the long run the truth does not matter". Now that's really the first line of the poem. So I write, "In the long run the truth does not matter", and then go on to investigate that. Because truth will be poetry and poetry is the one thing that cannot be corrupted.

(http://www.johnkinsella.org/interviews/adamson.html)

In my poem, the boat is flowing against the current, the swimlines are not those of the received speech patterns of "old-timers" of the river Adamson has so vividly scored in his own poetry, and that I have heard around the river on visiting him. In some ways, I feel it's harder to write against the line when lines are so clearly announced – that is, when they compile themselves in search of a chronological and event-linear format. I believe this is the case in the above version, with maybe the exception of "as if taking offence" – and there I have deleted the key "on their behalf", going for a more conventional ambiguity through tight expression – a lie I've re-admitted to the poem, and maybe in tune with issues of honesty and untruth in 'The Rumour', but antithetical to the drive of the poem.

On the web chat site I have referred to, my poem was cited as unredeemable "writing" (the title and first stanza – which remain the same across both versions – were not included, though a link to the *Jacket* URL containing the entire poem was), and its line breaks described as "radical" and sometimes "silly". The protest was against a supposed "modernist" urge towards creating lines of the same physical length, creating seemingly arbitrary line breaks which add nothing to meaning/sound etc. The general prosiness of contemporary poetry was deplored, and then the discussion sidetracked into contemporary poets being read solely by contemporary poets because of this. I have paraphrased this from memory, but think I have the basic gist of the arguments.

The idea that "radical line breaks" (to quote one of my critics) involve the breaking of units of common speech or expression and associative meaning might be allowed, I guess, in a kind of obvious declarative enjambment, where meaning carries over the line for a specific dramatic effect (and I'm all in favour of enjambment), or as an antidote to the repetitive staidness of the end-stopped line; in the same way that substitution of a foot in metrical verse brings relief to the reader and good opportunities for the poet to show how elastic set form really is. This is all good, but working within the shape and framework of the de-formalised poem one can, of course, go further. That's what interests me: keeping enough of the form for it to be recognised as coming out of some kind of "tradition", but radicalising enough to question the heritage and the need for variation itself. It's self-damning as much as "illuminating".

If we view the basic reason for line breaks as rhythmic, and rhythm in poetry as directly connected with mood and meaning, then it inevitably brings us to the question of what necessitates a particular rhythm in the first place. Back in the Western Australian wheatbelt, and surrounded by paddocks, I make use of my brother's full drum kit to vent some of my... er, rhythmic urges. Drumming can drive itself. You start with a basic four-four beat – common time – then maybe slip into doubles, then compound a three-four beat into a six-eight, a waltz to Spanish variations – and build from there and break away (you can frame anything, do it in any denomination you want); or you can listen to (or hear in your head) a piece of music and drum to it with the same principle. My brother drums to words – lineated and non-lineated!

Either way, the ability to keep time is the skill; the art comes in breaking free of that – to my mind at least. And I'm not only talking about jazz-like innovation – divergences that ultimately take you back to a point of reference – but rather the notes of discord or arrhythmia that genuinely contradict the form you are working in or through. It might be that one aspect remains consistent – the accent of the drumming, for instance – a little like the length of the line becoming the measure of rhythm rather than the integrity of speech grouping or associative meaning. In other words, the line forces us to hear what we wouldn't hear by reading for literally expressed meaning (even where it's "figurative") – it forces us to listen against expectation. It doesn't have to sound pleasing at first listening, but a different way of listening and thus hearing is suggested.

On the Microsoft Help and Support site on the web, the imperialism of correct expression finds its most paranoid and authentication-hungry expression. It's where the new media self-validate through the philanthropy of assistance and explication. It struck me: what of the line faltering between email packages – a common experience for poets and editors. "Because I have problems with lineation, I have marked the end of each line with..." Anyway, here's a little MS internationalism at work:

> OL2002: Posts Do Not Honor Line Breaks in Plain Text
> Format
> View products that this article applies to.
> Article ID : 287816
> Last Review : June 27, 2001
> Revision : 1.0
> This article was previously published under Q287816
>
> SYMPTOMS
> When you create a new plain text formatted post that contains line breaks, the line breaks are removed when the Auto Remove Line Breaks feature is enabled unless there are two successive line breaks. However, the posts do not display any indication that this has occurred, other than the change in formatting. The information bar message about extra line breaks does not appear, either in the Preview pane or when you read the post. This processing appears to happen when the message is initially posted.
>
> (http://support.microsoft.com/default.aspx?scid=kb;EN-US;q287816)

Experiencing this lapse in day-to-day emailing might mean confusion of meaning for the reader untried in the vagaries of email, but generally we'd be able to nut our way through it. For the poem – especially one that doesn't use capitalisation to begin a line – it offers a real problem: a probable defeat of the original intention behind the poem...? Or, even worse, a misreading that might lead to an accusation of shoddy craftsMANship. I WANT that software. I want my line breaks to falter and differ from recipient to recipient. One error in a book is just irritating, but a generative process that recreates text in an infinitely varied way is deeply appealing. It's probably as prescriptive as "syntactical and rhetorical boundaries" – the same line break "errors" for all or most recipients. The third party infiltrates the text, but it's just their word against yours. The reader is left disappointed, maybe, but the error has been built into their expectations, their adjusted sense of rhythm. The irony is, though we can with a skilled ear detect line breaks when verse is written in metrical stanzaic forms, and quite often in free verse, it's an extremely visual way of listening. There's nothing wrong with that, but rather than sight and sound interacting, it's more a demarcation of the two.

Gertrude Stein, in Stanza LXI (Part V) of *Stanzas In Meditation* (Sun & Moon, Los Angeles, 1994, p.201) wrote:

> I wish once more to mention
> That I like what I see.

We can hear that line break and don't really need to see the page. But knowing it's Gertrude Stein we might doubt it a little. Stein had an intense sense of the line (one non-believers called prosaic, despite its musicality), and where the expectation of a line break might be... broken. Seeing is to gain comfort. Milton's great sonnet of his blindness is a poem about seeing as much as loss of sight. Few poems embrace the blindness of the line, think outside the kind of drumming that simply keeps the beat. I've always admired Keith Richards's wise words about Charlie Watts, sublime drummer of the not-so-sublime Rolling Stones, that went along the lines of: "a lot of drummers have the rock, but Charlie has the roll..." The roll happens alongside the rhythm, and is part of it, but it's also the slippage between the lines. Something to aspire to, maybe.

So, to cut a long story short, here's the published version of the poem with its much-drafted line breaks:

And Everyone Gathered In Objection Yet Again
for Robert Adamson

And suddenly there was a presence,
as if it were worth something,
the pylons sticking up out of the water
like busted bones out of flesh.

A waterbird landed but didn't make
much of an impression – a damp squib
by comparison – though a couple
of fishermen couldn't take their

eyes off it. Bloody voyeurs
somebody muttered, and the bird,
as if taking offence on their behalf,
lifted and vanished into the confident

glow of the poem, the crowd
encrypting itself into the scene's
diffident colouration, troughed
and crested like the hum of the current.

(http://jacketmagazine.com/06/kins.html)

The poem itself occupies an indefensible position in terms of consistency in line breaks, but I stick by them and the means of getting to them – they were certainly more bothering to write than the first version shown above. I believe the poem gains in periphrasis, and though remaining fairly conventional in expression (it's not a paratactic poem, as such), the line breaks bring a suggestion of a dislocated clause structure. Readers are encouraged to read against expectation, to ironise their own process of reading through the poem ironising its own production. The observations have a sense of the matter-of-fact about them, even flatness (the "prosaic"?), a participation in the rumour that displaces the process of witness, telling and insight. A possibly frustrating characteristic of the poem, for anyone reading and expecting a certain kind of lineation, is that the poem is primarily lyrical, though it refuses to settle into the rises and fall of lyrical song rhythms. I would hope that the distraction and displacement of lyrical impetus makes the poem more volatile in its register, more evasive, and that as Andrew Zawacki noted in his *ABR* and *Notre Dame Review* piece, " 'And Everyone Gathered In Objection Yet Again' plies an eerie natural and aesthetic transfiguration..." (*Australian Book Review*, November 2000, Issue 226). In this case, the upsetting of the givens is as much a result of the "radical and silly line breaks", as it is about the words used.

What's it about? Maybe it's just about an unidentified (choice or lack?) water-bird – the lack of naming encrypting the rumour of it having been seen. So, the biggest irony for me is that "everyone gathered in objection yet again". Maybe that's the other point of the poem. I'm sure Jo Shapcott felt the same when, in the early years (late '90s) of the *Poetryetc* email discussion list, a well-known British avant-gardist denigrated Shapcott's astonishingly technically accomplished poetry as being inadequate because her line breaks were supposedly "without volition". Coming from a self-proclaimed innovator, this struck me as being rather imperceptive, or even hypocritical. Women poets often get the line break and form argument thrown at them – I say, thank goodness that some resist expectations of form and convention. If Joanna Russ had been a poet rather than a science fiction writer, she might have had a chapter in *How to Suppress Women's Writing* (The Women's Press, London, 1983), on the male policing (or "masculine" policing), of female line breaks. The gendered reading comes from the outside as much as from inside the poem-text. Lineation can easily become a security, a status quo, that needs, on occasion, to be resisted.

My partner, poet Tracy Ryan, wrote a response to the criticism of Jo Shapcott's line breaks as part of a series of poems entitled *bloc-notes*. I leave the last words to her:

Masterclass

You're nobody without prosody. Let me show you how it's done honey. I told the bitch, I said. I love her instinctive but without prosody, without volition. The definition of lack. I broke her line like a twig for her, like a waist so slender my hero hand could. Like a neck. Snap, a match like a rhyme. Tinder and flame, just begging for it. It wasn't force but you couldn't say consent. What she needs is a good enjambment. This thing is private. Lil ol me. The lines just lay down like that. Lil ol me. I have always relied on the kindness.

For John Kinsella's Articulated Coda to this essay, see inside back cover.

That Have Not Been Asked

Ten Dispatches about Endurance in Face of Walls

JOHN BERGER

1

> The wind got up in
> the night and took our plans away.
> (Chinese proverb)

2

The poor have no residence. They have homes because they remember mothers or grandfathers or an aunt who brought them up. A residence is a fortress, not a story; it keeps the wild at bay. A residence needs walls. Nearly everyone among the poor dreams of a small residence, like dreaming of rest. However great the congestion, the poor live in the open, where they improvise, not residences, but places for themselves. These places are as much protagonists as their occupants; the places have their own lives to live and do not, like residences, wait on others. The poor live with the wind, with dampness, flying dust, silence, unbearable noise (sometimes with both; yes, that's possible!), with ants, with large animals, with smells coming from the earth, rats, smoke, rain, vibrations from elsewhere, rumours, nightfall, and with each other. Between the inhabitants and these presences there are no clear marking lines. Inextricably confounded, they together make up the place's life.

"Twilight was setting in; the sky wrapped in cool grey fog was already being closed off by darkness; and the wind, after spending the day rustling stubble and bare bushes that had gone dead in preparation for winter, now laid itself down in still low places on the earth…"

The poor are collectively unseizable. They are not only the majority on the planet, they are everywhere and the smallest event speaks of them. This is why the essential activity of the rich today is the building of walls – walls of concrete, of electronic surveillance, of missile barrages, minefields, frontier controls, and opaque media screens.

3

The lives of the poor are mostly grief, interrupted by moments of illumination. Each life has its own propensity for illumination and no two are the same. (Conformism is a habit cultivated by the well-off.) Illuminated moments arrive by way of tenderness and love – the consolation of being recognised and needed and embraced for being what one suddenly is! Other moments are illuminated by an intuition, despite everything, that the human species serves for something.

"Nazar tell me something or other – something more important than anything.

"Aidym turned down the wick in the lamp in order to uses less paraffin. She understood that, since there was something or other in life that was more important than anything, it was essential to take care of every good that there was.

"'I don't know the thing that really matters, Aidym,' said Chagataev. 'I haven't thought about it, I've never had time. But if we've both of us been born, then there must be something in us that really matters.'

"Aidym agreed: 'A little that does matter... and a lot that doesn't.'

"Aidym prepared supper. She took a flat bread out of a sack, spread it with sheep's fat and broke it in half. She gave Chagataev the big half, and took the small half herself. They silently chewed their food by the weak light of the lamp. In the Ust-Yurt and the desert it was quiet, uncertain and dark."

4

From time to time despair enters into the lives which are mostly grief. Despair is the emotion which follows a sense of betrayal. A hope against hope (which is still far from a promise) collapses or is collapsed; despair fills the space in the soul which was occupied by that hope. Despair has nothing to do with nihilism.

Nihilism, in its contemporary sense, is the refusal to believe in any scale of priorities beyond the pursuit of profit, considered as the end-all of social activity, so that, precisely: everything has its price. Nihilism is resignation before the contention that Price is all. It is the most current form of human cowardice. But not one to which the poor often succumb.

"He began to pity his body and his bones; his mother had once gathered them together for him from the poverty of her flesh – not because of love and passion, not for pleasure, but out of the most everyday necessity. He felt as if he belonged to others, as if he were the last possession of those who have no possessions, about to be squandered to no purpose, and he was seized by the greatest, most vital fury of his life."

[A word of explanation about these quotations. They are from the stories of the great Russian writer, Andrei Platonov (1899–1951). He wrote about the poverty which occurred during the Civil War and later during the forced collectivisation of Soviet agriculture in the early 1930s. What made this poverty unlike more ancient poverties was the fact that its desolation contained shattered hopes. It fell to the ground exhausted, it got to its feet, it staggered, it marched on amongst shards of betrayed promises and smashed words. Platonov often used the term *dushevny bednyak*, which means literally poor souls. It referred to those from whom everything had been taken so that the emptiness within them was immense and in that immensity only their soul was left – that's to say their ability to feel and suffer. His stories do not add to the grief being lived, they save something. "Out of our ugliness will grow the world's heart", he wrote in the early 1920s.

The world today is suffering another form of modern poverty. No need to quote the figures; they are widely known and repeating them again only makes another wall of statistics. More than half the world's population lives with less than $2 a day. Local cultures with their partial remedies – both physical and spiritual – for some of life's afflictions are being systematically destroyed or attacked. The new technology and means of communication, the free market economy, productive abundance, parliamentary democracy, are failing, so far as the poor are concerned, to keep any of their promises beyond that of the supply of certain cheap consumerist goods, which the poor can buy when they steal.

Platonov understood living modern poverty more deeply than any other storyteller I have come across.]

5

The secret of storytelling amongst the poor is the conviction that stories are told so that they may be listened to elsewhere, where somebody, or perhaps a legion of people, know better than the storyteller or the story's protagonists what life means. The powerful can't tell stories: boasts are the opposite of stories, and any story however mild has to be fearless and the powerful today live nervously.

A story refers life to an alternative and more final judge who is far away. Maybe the judge is located in the future, or in the past that is still attentive, or maybe somewhere over the hill, where the day's luck has changed (the poor have to refer often to bad or good luck) so that the last have become first.

Story-time (the time within a story) is not linear. The living and the dead meet as listeners and judges within this time, and the greater the number of listeners felt to be there, the more intimate the story becomes to each listener. Stories are one way of sharing the belief that justice is imminent. And for such a belief, children, women and men will fight at a given moment with astounding ferocity. This is why tyrants fear storytelling: all stories somehow refer to the story of their fall.

"Wherever he went, he only had to promise to tell a story and people would take him in for the night: a story's stronger than a Tsar. There was just one thing: if he began telling stories before the evening meal, no-one ever felt hungry and he didn't get anything to eat. So the old soldier always asked for a bowl of soup first."

6

The worst cruelties of life are its killing injustices. Almost all promises are broken. The poor's acceptance of adversity is neither passive nor resigned. It's an acceptance which peers behind the adversity and discovers there something nameless. Not a promise, for (almost) all promises are broken; rather something like a bracket, a parenthesis in the otherwise remorseless flow of history. And the sum total of these parentheses is eternity.

This can be put the other way round: on this earth there is no happiness without a longing for justice.

Happiness is not something to be pursued, it is something met, an encounter. Most encounters, however, have a sequel; this is their promise. The encounter with happiness has no sequel. All is there instantly. Happiness is what pierces grief.

"'We thought there was nothing left in the world, that everything had disappeared long ago. And if we were the only ones left, what was the point of living?'

"'We went to check, said Allah. 'Were there any other people anywhere? We wanted to know.'

"Chagataev understood them and asked if this meant they were now convinced about life and wouldn't be dying any more.

"'Dying's no use,' said Cherkezov. 'To die once – now you might think that's something necessary and useful. But dying once doesn't help you to understand your own happiness – and no one gets the chance to die twice. So dying gets you nowhere.'"

7

"Whilst the rich drank tea and ate mutton, the poor were waiting for the warmth and for the plants to grow."

The difference between seasons, as also the difference between night and day, shine and rain, is vital. The flow of time is turbulent. The turbulence makes life-times shorter – both in fact and subjectively. Duration is brief. Nothing lasts. This is as much a prayer as a lament.

"[The mother] was grieving that she had died and forced her children to mourn for her; if she could have, she would have gone on living forever so that nobody should suffer on her account, or waste, on her account, the heart and the body to which she had given birth... but the mother had not been able to stand living for very long."

Death occurs when life has no scrap left to defend.

8

"It was as if she were alone in the world, free from happiness and sorrow, and she wanted to dance a little, right away, to listen to music, to hold hands with other people." [...]

They are accustomed to living in close proximity with one another, and this creates its own spatial sense; space is not so much an emptiness as an exchange. When people are living on top of one another, any action taken by one has repercussions on the others. Immediate physical repercussions. Every child learns this.

There is a ceaseless spatial negotiation which may be considerate or cruel, conciliating or dominating, unthinking or calculated, but which recognises that an exchange is not something abstract but a physical accommodation. Their elaborate sign languages of gestures and hands are an expression of such physical sharing. Outside the walls collaboration is as natural as fighting; scams are current, and intrigue, which depends upon taking a distance, is rare. The word 'private' has a totally different ring on the two sides of the wall. On one side it denotes property; on the other an acknowledgement of the temporary need of someone to be left, as if alone, for a while. Every site inside the walls is rentable – every square metre counted; every site outside risks to become a ruin – every sheltering corner counted.

The space of choices is also limited. They choose as much as the rich, perhaps more, for each choice is starker. There are no colour charts which offer a choice between one hundred and seventy different shades. The choice is close-up – between this or that. Often it is made vehemently, for it entails the refusal of what has not been chosen. Each choice is quite close to a sacrifice. And the sum of the choices is a person's destiny.

9

No development (the word has a capital D as an article of faith on the other side of the walls), no insurance. Neither an open future nor an assured future exists. The future is not awaited. Yet there is continuity; generation is linked to generation. Hence a respect for age, since the old are a proof of this continuity – or even a demonstration that once, long ago, a future existed. Children are the future. The future is the ceaseless struggle to see that they have enough to eat and the sometimes-chance of their learning with education what the parents never learnt.

"When they finished talking, they threw their arms around each other. They wanted to be happy right away, now, sooner than their future and zealous work would bring results in personal and in general happiness. The heart brooks no delay, it sickens, as if believing in nothing."

Here the future's unique gift is desire. The future induces the spurt of desire towards itself. The young are more flagrantly young than on the other side of the wall. The gift appears as a gift of nature in all its urgency and supreme assurance. Religious and community laws still apply. Indeed amongst the chaos which is more apparent than real, these laws become real. Yet the silent desire for procreation is incontestable and overwhelming. It is the same desire that will forage for food for the children and then seek, sooner or later, (best sooner) the consolation of fucking again. This is the future's gift.

10

The multitudes have answers to questions which have not yet been posed, and they have the capacity to outlive the walls.

The questions are not yet asked because to do so requires words and concepts which ring true, and those currently being used to name events have been rendered meaningless: Democracy, Liberty, Productivity, etc.

With new concepts the questions will soon be posed, for history involves precisely such a process of questioning. Soon? Within a generation.

Meanwhile, the answers abound in the multitudes' multiple ingenuities for getting by, their refusal of frontiers, their search for holes in the walls, their adoration of children, their readiness when necessary to become martyrs, their belief in continuity, their recurring acknowledgement that life's gifts are small and priceless.

Trace with a finger tonight her (his) hairline before sleep.

'I Would Softly Tell My Love' and 'That Have Not Been Asked' were included in the Spring 2005 catalogue, *Here is Where We Meet* (London: edited by Gareth Evans). We are grateful for the opportunity to publish them here.

REVIEWS

Writing is remembrance; but it is also forgetting, because an elegy suggests that the deceased is somehow put away in their proper place so that the elegist can move on.
—David Kennedy

Snatching at Beauty

PETER MCDONALD

J.H. Prynne, *Poems*, Freemantle Arts Centre Books / Bloodaxe Books,
£15.00, ISBN 1852246561

To begin with the obvious – even facile – point, the poetry of J.H. Prynne is not easy. In some ways, such an observation is true but useless: it begs too many questions, for example, about what 'easy' writing might actually be, and about why readers might want to be at ease with poetry like this, or want it to put them at their ease; more seriously, the often-made point places Prynne's verse in the kind of critical matrix ('easy'/'difficult') where most of its meaning – and all of its subtlety – are likely to be lost. In fact, *enjoying* Prynne's poetry is far easier than is generally suggested; indeed, the enjoyment, like the kinds of actual difficulty that come along with it, is very frequently unavoidable.

This new edition of Prynne's *Poems* updates the previous issue of 1999, supplementing it with six collections, the most recent of which (2004's *Blue Slides at Rest*) appears for the first time in this volume. A lot of the newer material is compelling, and it reveals a poet developing at a furious pace, whose sense of language and form is producing work of dazzling inventiveness and, yes, extreme strangeness. In *Pearls that Were* (1999), Prynne writes of "trivial deep amazement", and the phrase might well be applied to the kind of response his poetry makes possible, where the astonishing clutter and glitter of language that propels itself into the foreground of our attention seems at length to form its own shapes of depth and pattern. As throughout his career, Prynne continues to achieve these effects by means of a sense of line and sound which is, in its own way, intensely and memorably musical.

Pearls that Were itself exemplifies this. Untypically, Prynne relies here largely on quatrains; but these show all the more clearly a unique fineness, and lightness, of touch:

> Or so as softly we can laugh, as sure
>   and dear at every span
> in audit cry, extended memory address
>   translucent to the bone.

Freely bees awaken, rising to many tasks
  in jaunty flights forsaken, turning
enrolled to occupy their sentimental places
  and polish off their finer tuning.

Trace the residuals, the throng of men who
  surmount dative assignments
as if inching wildly, crazed for upper lights
  that flood what they want.

Upon the bed of rock, whose even smile remits
  its port in stormy air, her sight
not measured in the leaves of trembling ash
  that shade her face from thought.

It would take a good deal of critical courage to deny the beauty of this. While the section echoes and reconfigures motifs and images from the rest of the sequence, it also displays more self-containing kinds of design. Rhyme, employed with an extraordinary sureness of timing and suspension here, is perhaps complicit with the "sentimental" (as Prynne hints elsewhere): but the way in which its "turning" is accommodated to a "finer tuning" in this passage is certainly both haunting and unsettling. The language here is now so distinctive that – entirely without straining to be so – it could only be Prynne's: "translucent to the bone", like "inching wildly, crazed for upper lights", are phrases in an idiom which the rest of Prynne's poetry has brought to birth. In common with the best of the Modernist writing from which Prynne has drawn inspiration (though which, in fact, he seldom if ever imitates), this is a style which snatches at moments of beauty, order, or illumination while taking a pummelling from the energies and inertias of unstoppable language(s) in the contemporary world.

The full reach of this edition of *Poems* takes in those volumes of Prynne's which now look essential: from the brilliant assurance and balance of *Kitchen Poems* (1968), through the central achievements of *Brass* (1971) and *High Pink on Chrome* (1975), to later works of startling – and still bewildering – originality, notably *Down Where Changed* (1979) and *Her Weasels Wild Returning* (1994). Time and again, at all the stages of his career, Prynne manages to combine what we might think of as the agendas of experimentalism (fairly so, for many of the books seem almost excessively deliberate in their modelling and execution) with the capacity to deliver poetry (and, sometimes, poems) of focussed concentration and power. Prynne's diction can be almost forbiddingly scientific – in this, arguably, revealing the formative importance for him of poets like the early Auden and (especially) William Empson – while his sense of line is, from the very beginning, distinctively sharp. Whatever the difficulties of this poetry's content, its styles and forms are always distinctive and definite.

"Anyone who takes up this book," Prynne quotes in an epigraph of 1979, "will, we expect, have done so because at the back of his mind he has the half formed belief that there is something in it." The source, we are told, is *Practical Crystal-Gazing* (1916); and the wry humour of Prynne's quotation might obviously be applied to a volume like *Poems*. But too many readers of contemporary poetry are tempted by the complacent assumption that Prynne's work, like crystal-gazing, will not reward the attention it requires. If it contains much that is baffling, demanding, and discomforting, this collected volume also contains poetry of real strength, beauty and intricacy. *Poems* is that rare thing, a genuinely necessary book for anyone who pretends to an appreciation of modern British poetry.

Peter McDonald is Director of Tower Poetry, and Christopher Tower Student and Tutor in Poetry in the English Language at Christ Church, Oxford.

❧

Forms of Remembrance

DAVID KENNEDY

Stéphane Mallarmé, *For Anatole's Tomb*, Carcanet, £9.95, ISBN 1857546369,
trans. with an Introduction and Afterword by Patrick McGuinness;
Daniel Weissbort, *From Russian with Love: Joseph Brodsky in English*,
Anvil Press Poetry, £12.95, ISBN 0856463426;
Esther Morgan, *The Silence Living in Houses*,
Bloodaxe Books, £7.95, ISBN 1852247118;
Alan Ross, *Poems*, selected and introduced by David Hughes,
The Harvill Press, £18.99, ISBN 1843432242

Poetry consoles us with representation and recollection. The wistful endings that still characterise vast swathes of high street and competition verse allow us to celebrate our desire in the precise moment of finding it inoperative. This celebration flatters our intellectual vanity. It is at once complicit with capitalism *and* as old as Apollo, on seeing Daphne become a laurel, choosing to employ the metamorphosed object of his desire as a species of self-memorial. The myth tells us that poetry is synonymous with elegy, with the representation of loss. We are consoled because we can represent loss; it's what we expect from poetry. What happens when that expectation ceases to have any reality is one of the impulses behind *For Anatole's Tomb*.

In October 1879, Mallarmé's eight-year-old son died after several months of illness; and the poet's attempts to write a 'tombeau' in his memory resulted in 210 sheets of pencilled notes, unpublished until 1961. As Patrick McGuinness points out, these notes show a father's grief struggling with a poet's instincts. Mallarmé's attempts to write the poem amount to nothing less than an ontology of death and an anatomy of the desire to write the unendurable:

> Death – whispers softly – I am no one…my beauty is made up
> of *last moments* – lucidity, beauty face – of what would be me
> – without me – for as soon as I am – (that one dies) I cease to
> be…

> *

> Oh! you know that if I consent to live – to seem to forget you
> – it is to feed my pain – so that this seeming forgetting – may
> spring forth more painfully in tears…

Writing is remembrance; but it is also forgetting, because an elegy suggests that the deceased is somehow put away in their proper place so that the elegist can move on. Mallarmé's notes look forward to all those twentieth-century writers who have feared that writing to commemorate the unspeakable will become a second death. It is a fear audible in Wilfred Owen's 'I am not concerned with Poetry' or in Paul Celan's polysemic and often negative neologisms. However, neither Owen nor Celan *expected* loss to be their cultural dominant. We, on the other hand, live in the age of built-in loss – from products that may help save the planet to "your home is at risk if you do not keep up payments on a loan secured against it". So the question is whether poetry can do anything else than reproduce the dominant. Reading *For Anatole's Tomb* is not only a moving experience but also a profoundly chastening one because it reminds us what is at stake not only in the writing of poetry but in assuming language can represent the world. Patrick McGuinness's excellent parallel text edition should be required reading on all creative writing courses.

Daniel Weissbort's book is subtitled *Pages from a Journal 1996-97*. It selects from what he terms a "hotchpotch" of responses to Joseph Brodsky's death. What results is simultaneously a work of mourning, imbricated as such works always are with "self-interrogation and speculation"; "a kind of posthumous discussion with Joseph"; and "a kind of meditation on the poetics of translation". That double "kind of" allows Weissbort to leave various generic doors ajar and ask questions that elegists rarely open: "how many of us made you who you were?" and "how many of us did you make who we are?" These are important questions in relation to a Nobel Laureate, a representative and producer of what Weissbort terms somewhere "world culture", because they push open others: what kind of poet was Brodsky or did people want him to be? *and* what kind of project was the translation of poetry from behind the Iron Curtain? Works often get translated because they embody things that either don't exist in the target language or which, crucially, its speakers can't allow themselves to have. The Iron Curtain translation project did both. Poets writing about universals or celebrating individualism were persecuted. This made their work political: which in turn enabled these types of poem to be revalidated at a time when Western poets were losing confidence in them. The brand values of heroic, romantic poetry were remarketed. Moreover, Brodsky's remark, in an interview with Willam Walsh reprinted in *Talking Verse* (Verse, 1995), that attempts to expand the canon are "pure bunk" which have only a "therapeutic-narcissistic value", suggests "world culture" might be about reactionary views somehow purified by persecution.

Brodsky seems to have delighted in both playing up to and contradicting his own legend, so *From Russian with Love* reads largely as an account of a struggle over Brodsky's identity. For example, Weissbort worries about his Jewishness and what he really felt about it. Similarly, he quotes liberally from a range of critics who disliked Brodsky's own translations of his poetry. Weissbort's book is "a kind of" elegy and elegies are always struggles with identity. But the chorus arguing over Brodsky's 'authentic' voice reveals just how much was at stake in the Iron Curtain translation project. Translation has, it seems to me, the biggest cash and status earning potential in poetry; and Weissbort gives a fascinating insight into a poetry 'class fraction' jetting from seminar to conference and having self-important conversations about translation and nationality. The book has its own conversation with Brodsky's poem 'May 24, 1980'. Different versions do tell us a lot about translation but the poem itself makes Brodsky's reputation hard to fathom.

Esther Morgan's second collection offers three different interpretations of its epigraph from Alice Monro – "[a woman] is the house; there is no separation possible". In 'The House Of', female ghosts and a present female owner haunt each other. The speaker of these seventeen, generally short, lyrics is restless and sleepless, watchful of her own perceptions of minute changes in her surroundings. In contrast, the ghosts seem purposeful, grounded in nightly routines. The poems are so concerned with portraying the ineffable that they often seem semi-actualized. The best pieces – 'Domestic', 'Poppies' – allow images to become strange stories. The title section comprises eighteen poems, in a similar style, that tell the story of an abusive relationship from which the woman finally escapes. The two sections share a vocabulary of beds, night, bones, mirrors and broken china but 'The Silence Living in Houses' adds images of meat, flesh and animals to replace the first section's generalized unease with the terror of actual events and behaviours. The final section, 'Are You Homesick for the House of Cards?', measures the speaker's life against those of her mother and grandmother. These poems are more alive because they are full of the material world – sweets, food, furniture – in active use. They are also full of echoes of the first section. There are, for example, rusted locks in both. "My mother moved through the house like a priest" looks back to "I make my last round at midnight". Similarly, looking into "late-night mirrors" and finding a kind of ancestry looks back to the restless woman at the ghost's "dressing-table triptych /…trying to catch… / the flit of a face." This has the curious effect of making the last section seem nostalgic for the time when women had definite roles to escape from; and of making the first section read as if contemporary female identity is somewhere between vacant self-possession and narcissism. The patterning of the book and the scarcity of striking individual poems do seem to invite us to read it as a cumulative document.

David Hughes's selection from the late Alan Ross's poetry also works cumulatively. Organized thematically, not chronologically, it begins and ends with poems about the Second World War. This is highly appropriate for a body of work which keeps returning to that conflict and whose practice rarely strays far from the middle of the twentieth century. The voice of Ross's poems is similar to those we hear in Keith Douglas, Bernard Spencer or early Roy Fuller. These poets, like the sailors in Ross's 'Heligoland', "critically take stock". The adverb acts like extra insurance against suddenly failing to be unillusioned. Remembering how my late father and father-in-law – both veterans – used to speak, it occurs to me that the Second World War produced a voice that the poets merely recorded but in doing so made into *the* voice of the period. It was not the other way round. Cool, journalistic observations accumulate easily into poems that are then reined in by uneasy skepticism: "something (but what?) could be made of this". There are rather too many cricket and travel poems here, which nearly obscure what that something is. As Ross notes in 'Student Riots in the Middle East', "causes evaporate; just the dead persist." The persistence of the dead demands that we perpetually revalue our relation to them. The poet's mind, like the oceans in 'The Sea, 1939-45', moves restlessly between "disaster", "assurance" and "the tides of compassion". This, too, derives from that mid-century poetic, so that the rejection of poetically easy valuations and consequent perpetual unsettling and resettling of representation become a scrupulous form of remembrance.

David Kennedy's latest collection is *The Roads* (Salt, 2004). Books on Douglas Dunn and on elegy are forthcoming from Northcote House and Routledge respectively.

❧

We Think We Are Living Now

JAN MONTEFIORE

Anne Stevenson, *Poems 1955-2005*, Bloodaxe, £12.00, ISBN 1852246995; Rita Ann Higgins, *Poems Selected and New*, Bloodaxe, £9.95, ISBN 1852247002

Anne Stevenson's collected poems, spanning half a century, have an impressive range and variety: the book comprises lyrics, monologues, meditative poems, poems of memory, representing a lifetime's dedication to the art of words, meaning both the power of poetry to net in its language the lives of humans subjected to time – whose remorseless passing undoes their acts and selves even as they conceive them – and the singing lines and stanzas whose melodies contain such losses and absences. As she writes in 'The Fiction Makers', her elegy for Frances Horowitz, poets are as subject to time as any other mortal:

> Out of pink-cheeked Cwmdonkin,
> Dylan with his Soho grin.
> Planted in the fiercest of flames
> gold ash on a stem.
> When Henry jumped out of his joke,
> Mr Bones sat in.
> Even you, with your breakable heart
> in your ruined skin,
> those poems all written
> that have to be you, dear friend,

you guessed you were dying now,
but you were dying then.

Most of Stevenson's gifts are here: the easy yet deeply serious engagement with the traditions of modernist writing, inflected by a sharp awareness of the paradoxical status of any 'tradition' of modernism; the personal warmth for the lost friend; and the music of the lyrical refrain mourning all those, including the poet herself, who "thought we were living now/ but we were living then".

Anne Stevenson's musicianship is everywhere visible in her poetry, especially in her handling of rhyme and refrain; she excels at what Hopkins calls the "counterpoint" of free conversational speech rhythms running across recognisable melody and contained or closed by rhymes whose harmony makes tolerable the aching loss that is the subject of so many poems. That feeling for the music of language has driven her fierce attack on the appropriation of poetry by 'identity politics', as she has written in essay 'Defending the Freedom of the Poet':

> Without wishing to dissociate myself from the politics of feminism or from any anger at social injustice that has pricked the consciences of many people in the post-war years, as a poet I have to question the wisdom of linking poetry with political movements of any kind [...] How can a multiplicity of jostling, incongruous, historically produced texts be bundled up under a gendered and, especially in our time, emotively pressured appellation?

The initial caveat is important: Stevenson is not arguing for poetry to be regarded as apolitical universal transcendence, any more than she is repudiating feminist politics. This collection includes several strikingly sharp political poems, including the distinctly feminist 'Ballad of Made Maid' who would "sooner lose my maidenhead / Than lose my maiden name" and sends a would-be dominant male packing: "If you think I will be led / Into your baited shrine, / You'd better find a maiden bred / In eighteen eighty-nine". And of course feminism is strongly present in her justly-celebrated 1974 sequence 'Correspondences', epistolary poems which trace four generations of the New England Chandler family: whose complacent males lay down the law to their intellectually aspiring, dutifully submissive but inwardly dissenting women, the terse eloquence of whose words can become poetry only through Stevenson's creation of their imaginary letters, journals and unpublished poems. Revisiting this sequence, I was struck afresh by its sharp, angry portrayal of gender relations. None of the Chandler males, whether Calvinist minister, successful businessman, liberal progressive or 1960s hippy, thinks for a moment of questioning his own self-righteous certainties, while the far more intelligent and aspiring wives and daughters question their own aspirations to the point of paralysis and consequently never live up to their own potential – at least until the youngest daughter of the family chooses to abandon her wifely and daughterly duties in the US for an independent life as the poet "Kay Boyd" in London (whom inevitably one interprets as an autobiographical *alter ego*), whose meditations on the impossibility of writing the truth end the sequence.

But of course *Correspondences* is not *only* a chronicle of wasted talents through a history of the decline of New England puritan idealism within the larger history of the United States from 1830. An important aspect of Anne Stevenson's poetry is engagement with traditions – both the tradition of American idealism and independence in which she was brought up (which possibly inspired some of the sharper poems about English cosiness and the passivity of nice English women), and the traditions of European music and of English poetry. These are invoked, never obediently and often obliquely, in poems about players of Schubert and Beethoven; teachers and John Keats; the many poems dedicated to fellow poets such as Norman MacCaig, John Heath-Stubbs (the witty 'Spring Poem', affectionately mimicking his own style in a celebration of spring cleaning); the ambivalent but ungrudging poems to Plath "the fiercest poet of our time"; the beautiful 'Willow Song' (another elegy for Frances Horowitz) whose title though not its theme deliberately echoes Shakespeare; and the late monologues, like that of the disabled painter in 'Red Hot Sex'; or the aged Jewish doctor in 'The Name of the Worm' who recalls his young wife in the 1930s discomfiting a pushy Nazi anglophile who:

> kept quoting Shakespeare, knew a bit of Chaucer,
> and to prove it one morning, presented Margaret with a rose.
> Now Margaret, fair-skinned with auburn hair, was in those
> days lovely, but her politics were redder than her hair:
> *Oh rose thou art sick, and the name of the worm is Hitler –*

This moment of female energy and Blakean anger exploding into humdrum conversation makes an oblique but important point about the power of words "whose action is no stronger than a flower", of which the range and variety of these poems constitutes an impressive proof. The only real flaw in the book is its arrangement: rather than the usual method of arranging poems either chronologically or in order of published collections, the author has chosen a thematic arrangement according to subjects like place, or human life at different ages, or death, or the art of poetry. This is an appropriate strategy for single collections, but in a book of 400 pages, which simply contains too many poems to make effective correspondences, it becomes irritating. The thematic categories often overlap, so that the placing of poems seems arbitrary, and the temporal mix-up makes it impossible to 'watch' the poet's development through time. That said, this is a splendid and rich collection, and a bargain at £12.

Rita Ann Higgins, inhabiting a very different terrain from Stevenson's Ann Arbor, Oxford, Wales and Durham, has made a rhetoric out of the life and language of the Irish working class, not unlike a feminine and politicised poetic answer to Roddy Doyle's fiction; the speakers of her dramatic monologues are more likely to be preoccupied with their hairstyles or *Eastenders* or how to pay the rent than with Blake or Shakespeare. Her lyrics of working-class life and women's experiences have a splendid liveliness, energy and affection, as with the celebration of pious Catholic mothers, praying

> We adore thee O Christ we bless thee
> Because by thy cross thou hast redeemed the world
>
> Sincere pleas to Jesus, that the eldest might
> get off with a light sentence, pledges of no more smoking [...]

Higgins, who has been rightly praised for her "stylised colloquialisms", has always been good at riffing on the spoken word; hers is more a poetry of the spoken voice to be listened to than the written page to be puzzled over. Her later poems are equally sympathetic to the dispossessed but more sardonic about the poetry world, as in 'The Clemson Experience' where golf coaching meets a conference on Irish literature "where they heaney time by plucking out the maggots / and sucking the marrow out of the bones of the bogmen of Ireland", or the 'After Dinner Speaker' who incautiously demands a fee from the President of the Galway's Business and Professional Women's Club: "She fell into her crystal shop with shock." Higgins is a poet who almost always surprises and refreshes by her energy and sympathy, to which the most recent poems add an increasing allusive range. Very different from Anne Stevenson, the two nevertheless share the distinction of creating an exhilaratingly discomfiting poetry.

Jan Montefiore 's books include *Feminism and Poetry: Language, Identity, Experience in Women's Writing*

FEATURE REVIEW
Prose by Three Women Poets

MICHELENE WANDOR

Bernadine Evaristo, *Soul Tourists*, Hamish Hamilton, £12.99, ISBN 024114115X;
Ruth Padel, *Tigers in Red Weather*, Little, Brown, £17.99, ISBN 0316726001;
Elaine Feinstein, *Anna of All the Russias*,
Weidenfeld & Nicolson, £20, ISBN 0297643096

In principle, there is no reason to think that prose written by poets should warrant special attention, either in their approach to the writing or in a critical approach to the reading. Evidence of sensitivity to language, in whatever form, should be paramount in the work of any professional writer. However, there are always going to be fruitful ways of teasing out the relationship between prose and poetry, and these three books afford a good opportunity to do so.

Poetry figures as part of the content of all three books, but in rather different ways. Elaine Feinstein, herself a fine novelist as well as a poet and translator, adds to her credentials as biographer in this lucid and compelling book about the life and work of Anna Akhmatova. As well as contextualising and commenting on Akhmatova's poetry, Feinstein uses the poems as a way of gaining deeper insight into the poet's life: reading the poems as autobiography. There can be problems in this kind of approach, I think, but Feinstein is so careful to mine all other possible sources – letters, diaries, interviews – for clues, that the poems become only one part of the evidence, rather than being read as the exclusive 'truth'.

Ruth Padel's book is part travelogue, part anthropology, part convincingly-presented arguments for wildlife conservation – and tucked almost shyly within the action-packed and evocative chapters is a fragment of memoir. Round India, Nepal, Bhutan, Russia and China, Malaya and other countries, she travels in search of the sights and sounds of tigers of all shapes and sizes. This book is an education, a twenty-first century equivalent of those amazingly detailed volumes produced by British travellers in the nineteenth century. As part of her armoury of associations, Padel is sensitive to the ways in which the tiger is part of our imaginative iconography; the figure of brave Bagheera from Kipling's *Jungle Book* is invoked, along with the ways in which unchecked human sexuality can be characterised as tiger-like. Poems by Donne, Blake, Dickinson and others are quoted, and appear complete in an appendix, to demonstrate the variety of poetic impulses the tiger has generated.

But there is also an interesting way in which the 'tiger' metaphor takes on a life of its own within the structure of Padel's narrative. Early in the book she refers to the end of a relationship, and as she travels to and from the sources of tiger-watching, back in London 'he' keeps popping up – at literary parties, at the ends of chapters, and occasionally as a brief interlude within a chapter. It is almost as if he – or his memory – stalks Padel, as she in turn stalks the real animals. This subtly-built metaphor, having veined the book, finally comes to rest when, seemingly free from his stifling influence, she writes "The person he had been with me was an endangered species".

Bernardine Evaristo, writing without the imperatives of either the biography or travelogue/anthropology, takes a revelling freedom. Her novel is picaresque in terms of both form and content. Following his father's death, Stanley lights out with girl-friend Jessie on a meandering journey round Europe, North Africa, and even further afield. This novel is a story about belonging and not belonging. When Jessie first appears in the novel, her voice is contained in free-verse poems. As the characters travel, so does the language. Fragments of dialogue, impressionistic prose paragraphs, unpunctuated sections of prose, pastiche newspaper interviews, almost metric couplets, and forays into the past which springs alive when invoked: all these accumulate to create lives in search. An eighteenth century seraglio eavesdrops on the present. Nothing is resolved, nothing ends. The journey, clearly, continues beyond the pages of the novel. The characters continue to search, for each other as well as their own selves, and the novel's tropism towards closure is denied by Evaristo's mix of forms.

Padel's book also has no real resolution. The story of the tiger in the modern world can have no ending – and certainly will have no end, unless the various campaigns for conservation, which she tracks, fail. This is, in the end, a campaigning book, carried along on the voice of someone who has braved hardship and personal difficulty to get close to the experiences which she wants to preserve – glancingly mirrored by an experience of which she wants to be, as it were, shot. Emotional exorcism has become a (perhaps) autobiographical by-product of an expedition into strange lands.

Of the three books, Feinstein's is the most indebted to recognisable conventions. This is partly because she takes her responsibilities to the life of another – her subject – as her main imperative. The 'Russias' of the title stretch from pre-Revolutionary Russia, through the Soviet Union, and out of Stalinism into post-Cold War Europe. Like her own country's, Akhmatova's fortunes as woman and poet ebb and flow. Serious love affairs with three compelling and oppressive men punctuate her life; her son Lev, enduring horrific imprisonment after an emotionally tortuous early life, ends up at odds with his mother. Above all, Feinstein evokes the paradox at the centre of her subject's life. While surviving as one of Russia's most important poets, most of her life seems to have been lived in poverty, travelling with a battered suitcase, haunted by recurring illnesses. Yet an honorary degree from Oxford University in 1965, the year before her death, attested to her importance to the non-Soviet West.

The use of metaphor, structural and symbolic, an openness to playing with form, a sensitivity to the uses of poetry within, and in relation to, prose – all these are features of all three books. However, as I said at the start, these are qualities which other writers have too, even if they don't make their reputations primarily as poets. What is particularly pleasing about this triumvirate is that they demonstrate that being a poet does not preclude political and cultural understanding, interest in the lives of others, or commitment to research and narrative. These ivory towers never lose sight of the real world or the worlds of other fictions.

Michelene Wandor holds a Royal Literary Fund Fellowship at Birkbeck College; and her new poetry collection, *Musica Transalpina*, is a Poetry Book Society Recommendation for Spring, 2006.

∂

ONE THAT GOT AWAY

The first in an occasional series in which recent books which missed adequate review on first publication are re-assessed.

Chorus and Eternal Return

ANDREW DUNCAN

John Hartley Williams, *Blues*, Cape, £9.00, ISBN 0224073443

In 'Dan Dare at the Cosmic Ballroom', the clean-cut English space hero (from a strip in *The Eagle* comic which I used to read in the 1960s) lands on Venus and meets his arch-enemy The Mekon, only to find that this is the planet of love:

> Welcome to the planet
> humans dream of on their cold blue ball.
> Welcome to the temperature of pleasant being.
> Dispel colonial ideas.

He goes through a door into a lurching ground of a million false perspectives, a labyrinth above a fall:

> From vertigo, the chorussing abyss
> reiterates its roundelay of little death:
> La-la again. La-la again. La-la again.

Next, he has a close encounter with Venusian green tea. His next adventure involves the waitress, and breaking the most basic rule of spaceman training – don't jump the species barrier. "She puts out tentacles. They slide between my ribs, / Dote upon the organs they encounter. / My pump begins its agonising pump. / She slips a duct into my sac of seed / and instantly replenishes my emptying. / *Once the circuit's made,* she whispers, / *it's unbreakable.*" He lies back and thinks of Earth: and there he is – in a simulation run by The Mekon's IT. In the virtual planet (or is it the real one?), which turns out to be a park where Time is the theme, midget dinosaurs sniff at his boots, a million quantum-entangled Dan Dares hop around. At the bottom of the mountain Dare breaks into a dance with the Dionysiac *corps de ballet* there, strips, plunges into the sea, and feels the perfect sensation of Home.

Williams is radically original, and constantly remaking himself. But we could float the idea of him as an Eastern European poet, one of the heroic breed who have abandoned hope in causes and instead are always interesting; who rely on individuality and on the vigour of folklore. Fellini got out of *neorealismo* through the comic strips (*fumetti*) of 'Lo Sceicco Bianco', and he haunts this comic-strip poem: but Fellini may have influenced modern Eastern European styles, especially in cinema. A closer equivalent to Williams's work might be the films of the ex-Yugoslav Emir Kusturica. (A valuable text in an earlier book, *Ignoble Sentiments*, describes experiences as a teacher in Belgrade. There is a hint that J.H. Williams in Serbia may have been a try-out for Dan Dare on Venus.)

Williams has a complete grasp of cutting-to-action and never decelerating. It's like the technique of painting on a bowl – once you've got it, the rhythm doesn't come to an end. This is one of the folklore aspects of his work: heroes in folklore never pay the bill, never run out of adventures, never stop for a seminar. It's not unlike the Endless Highway rambling of the

Blues – and makes most of the poetry I review look didactic and bureaucratic.

The influences of Baroque painting are not totally absent from either Fellini or Eastern European cinema; and its notion of trick perspective may help us to grasp Williams' prodigious technique, the combination of dislocated verticals and legend. Poems about the elbow, the ankle and the sneeze (or, forcible lyric ejaculation) show a distortion of normal proportions – a super-realism. Translated to the topology of a plot, this entails the ability to suggest a thousand paths.

'Not Till the Last Saxophone' offers an explanation of the book's title:

> Snowflakes big as tongues
> feel with a blur for your eyes
> (...)
> onward, friend,
> to the town where eternity becomes fashionable,
> where trains have not been seen in weeks.
> This is it boy. The blues
> hoist your bag better on your shoulders
> (...)
> These are the long, cold deepwalking drifts

where the protagonist trudges through a world of pain into folklore, into an unbreakable circuit, into vagrancy and a music where "Stars are a Hammond organ, / solo hailstones, / hard on the roof of your head." Every tonal value is vivid, heightened, naive. The camera can be a documentary tool, or the channel for dreams: and Williams has mastered the quality of dream where everything flows and everything makes sense even in the middle of panic fear, erotic cloudbursts, losing your handhold on the sky and falling.

'Sarajevo Dancing' is an account of collective violence in Bosnia, rendered through tags from Serbian heroic songs and through the image of the *kolo*, the circle dance. With arms linked you have to go as fast as everyone else, and stay in step. This loss of individuality is a poetic analogy for hysteria. The *kolo* represents the triumph of community; and the community in question here massacred its neighbours. Amazingly, the poetry matches up to its material: the poem starts serenely and gradually accelerates into delirium, voices from heaven, fantasies of mutilation:

> Lazar, the choice is yours / a heavenly or an earthly kingdom.

Andrew Duncan edits *Angel Exhaust*. His latest book is *The Imaginary in Geometry*.

Writing With Light

DAVID MORLEY

Pigs Might Fly, John Heath-Stubbs, Carcanet Press, £7.95, ISBN 1857548191;
New Collected Poems, W.S. Graham, Faber, £16.99, ISBN 0571209890

There is panache to literary endurance. The recent poems of Les Murray, Charles Tomlinson, Peter Scupham and John Heath-Stubbs all bear marks of rapid, concentrated writing: a fast-focus vision; expert craft; and adeptness about the knowledge of the poem's time. They work at the top of their game. Natural talents, and the ability to learn, play a strong role in literary development, but character and stamina determine whether one lasts as a writer – as we will see in the case of W.S. Graham.

Some poets grow freer as they get older. For some, the incubation and gestation times for writing speed up, several poems running through their cognitive assembly lines simultaneously. The apprenticeship is long over, yet they write with the ease of beginners. Mellowing – even literary mellowing – is thought of by some as virtuous, as is the damnation of geniality. Both are manipulative legislations foisted by young writers on their elders to seize the game off them. I like my older poets fierce, frosty and restless. I like their example of hard work and curiosity. No pagefright for them.

For many such poets, mellowing can be safely left to younger writers who have not yet registered that making it work might be a more revolutionary aim than making it new. It is as if the November of a writing life leaves little time for much in the way of what Keats called *agonie ennuyeuse* (the tedious agony) – the fallowness of creativity before the storm of creation. The colour of these poets' voices grows tighter and tougher given a backwash of snow. Geoffrey Hill's recent progressions are exemplary in this respect. So are those of John Heath-Stubbs (born 1918) in his latest collection *Pigs Might Fly*:

> The sky was full of *cochons*.
> As they soared and swerved and swooped,
> Exactly by what means I could not discern.
> That was many years ago. I am an old man now,
> And the sight's so familiar
> That I am told people don't look up now as they once did.

This is not a tone of voice so much as a tone of mind: the mind engages its own mortality in a porcelain language, language that is firm, but does not conceal the inherent breakability in its making. In late life, great poets and novelists can achieve that cold and clarifying self-characterization: experience and ceaseless practice demand it of the voice. The effect of such self-characterization is not self-dramatization, it is a forensic honesty, and it is merciless. The poet achieves a coldness and frankness of expression and exposition that is largely unavailable to either the writer who lives in the moment and in his or her appetites, or one who cannot help thinking too much. You hear this voiceprint in Mandelstam's exile poems; you listen for it colouring Hardy's late poems. Here is the whole of Heath-Stubbs's 'In the Porcelain Factory'. Listen to the sound of its simple argument: the clarifying veneer of prose, the spoken assurance of line:

> Once I was shown around a porcelain factory,
> One of our best English producers of fine china
> But what I remember best is a small man –
> Hunchbacked he seemed or deformed in some way.
> His only task to paint images of birds on cups and saucers.
> This he did constantly and continually,
> Not pausing to notice those of us who gazed at him.
> I do not know if there was anyone to love him or to care for him.
> His whole life this constant repetition
> Of small images of love and song and freedom.
> He must be gone now and who will remember him?

Heath-Stubbs' task, in this book, is to paint small images, remembrances. What veers wonderfully in them are freedom, song, love. Like form, awareness of mortality is no prison to creation. You write against it: its restriction. It is as liberating as the knottiest of forms, despite the sensation that it makes time weigh upon the act of writing. But that weight is not just the weight of expectation, it is the weightless pleasure of action, however futile, however unseen or overlooked.

W.S. Graham's work was in peril of being overlooked – once. There were poets to love him and care for his work. Audiences do not wait; you must create them. Graham was not especially good at this in his life – but his poetry is capable of creating audience, and his advocates are out in the field. As you can damn by faint praise, so you can by over-praise: Graham's supporters are very canny in this respect; like water falling on stone, they have been very steady, persistent without becoming relentless.

I have given slightly more space to Heath-Stubbs because the W. S. Graham *New Collected Poems* is the paperback version of the 2004 hardcover, skillfully edited by Matthew Francis, a volume widely and positively reviewed last year. Graham's reputation has recovered from a position of inflicted and self-inflicted neglect. As Douglas Dunn writes in the Foreword, "Steadfastness of supporters (and the steadfastness, the indestructibility of the work) have led to Graham's reappearance…". His importance to poets, however, must be widened beyond that persuasive, persistent community. The task of recuperation is only half-complete: Graham still needs to gain more general readers, readers who are not academics or fellow writers. They deserve him. He writes with light.

It cannot be helped that fashion shadows our perception of writing. Reappraisals rot into neglect; favouritisms deform into denunciations. Writers tend not to be so fickle in their admirations (Dunn and Francis have been staunch), and general readers have far greater fidelity to a name. Literary quality, if the writer is lucky, outlasts any phase of cultural fashion. The panache of literary endurance fails without near-constant advocacy. I hope this volume is not a signal that the campaign is considered completed, the fashion mellowing, and that luck is, again, on the wane.

Of course, Graham is everything his reviewers claim: a canonical modernist romantic. There are few poems from the late twentieth century in English lovelier in their soundscapes than 'The Nightfishing' and 'Malcolm Mooney's Land'; few poems more agonizingly haunting than 'Loch Thom'; or darker and wiser than 'Johann Joachim Quantz's Five Lessons'. His language is beautifully turned for the ear, for he also writes with sound. That resonance will draw readers ever more closely. I propose Faber release on CD any recordings which Graham may have made, or commission a CD of the poems read by his steadfast poet-supporters. Include this recording in the next edition of the paperback. In the meantime, read these poems aloud to others. Poets: include one Graham poem in your own readings. You might deserve (you might need) the same advocacy one of these days.

David Morley's next collection, *The Invisible Kings*, is due from Carcanet in 2007.

Poetry Review 95:3

Due to a problem with our printing service which was beyond our control, some readers unfortunately received defective copies of *Poetry Review*, 95:3 'Underworld'. Please let us know if the binding of your copy is faulty and we will be happy to replace it.

Tel: 020 7420 9881 Email: membership@poetrysociety.org.uk

"Tomato is so vulgar and lustful…"

ROBYN BOLAM

Pascale Petit, *The Huntress*, Seren, £7.99, ISBN 1854113968;
Sarah Wardle, *Score!*, Bloodaxe, £7.95, ISBN 1852247061;
Jane Yeh, *Marabou*, Carcanet, £6.95, ISBN 1857547888;
Valentina Polukhina and Daniel Weissbort, eds.,
An Anthology of Contemporary Russian Women Poets,
Carcanet, £14.95, ISBN 1857547411

Pascale Petit's sequel to *The Zoo Father* is a brave and unsettling collection about a daughter's relationship with her mentally ill mother. In the opening poem the reader is invited to "Come in, and see / what no-one has witnessed". Here, the mother is metamorphosed into a "big palomino mare" full of snake venom, while in 'My Mother's Mirror', an Alice-like daughter is swallowed by the mirror and falls down a well inside it. This then becomes the throat of a serpent to which she has been sacrificed. The tiny rodent in 'Her Mouse Daughter' bites the neck of a rattlesnake mother who is eager to feed on her.

These are psychological explorations of relationships and power struggles that take risks: the daughter enters the mother's distorted world to fight violently for her own survival. In a six page poem, 'At the Gate of Secrets', she is transformed into a stag for protection and her mother's dependency is imaginatively perceived: "Only you know how to herd the chairs / so they stop butting me with their horns". The daughter's final promise to meet in the grave "where we will torment one another. / And no one else will suffer / as you will suffer then, my mother", is chilling.

Several poems seem steeped in pain, particularly 'The Summoner', with its raw detail of a sick woman's final debris set against her daughter's perception of her as "the snake head that even decapitated / will still have the reflex to bite me". Scenes are often surreal, but Pascale Petit can also convey a realistic presence powerfully, as she does in 'My Mother's Perfume': "her scent got so strong, I could taste the coins in the bottom of her handbag". This is a disturbing but fascinating third collection.

Sarah Wardle is poet-in-residence with Spurs F.C.: *Score!* is her second collection. In it, she moves from a eulogy to former manager, Bill Nicholson, to a loosely-rhymed sonnet celebrating Spurs forward, Defoe, and some quatrains 'after Heaney' for fellow striker, Keane (with an echo of Armitage), through a range of Spurs poems to the hard-hitting and wider-ranging

'Kabul'. Here, an athletics stadium is both the place of "the Taleban's first public execution / of a woman" and the space in which "girls are now playing football and celebrate… shooting at fate".

In 'Easter X', Wardle kicks off the last of ten variations on the sonnet form by re-writing Shakespeare's 'seven ages of man' speech from *As You Like It* ("A man in his time may be striker and manager") – ending a sequence that encompasses politics, religion, war and society with the fusion of football and poetry: "with each signing heading and kicking at goal/ on the birthing pitch, testing iambic feet, / in training for next season's final minute". Elsewhere, poets are encouraged to be those who can "curl it like Keane" or "risk it like Rednapp and bust a gut" rather than those who "stand on the sidelines, despair, give up".

Even when she isn't writing about football, Wardle often runs skilfully with phrases as if dribbling a ball towards the goal mouth. Her record here is thirty-two lines in 'Premonition', where she manages a new twist on the maternal anxiety dream poem when the daughter "playing in the castle grounds of her sub-conscious" is exposed to various novel threats and eventually "ends up in the sack / with the toad, who squats at the water's edge". *Score!* is a fine follow-up to Sarah Wardle's first collection, *Fields Away*. Imaginatively playful and technically experimental, it combines humour ("He strikes a pose… serene / as the Mona Lisa with a spliff" – 'The Female Gaze') with a flair for applying language sensuously.

At thirty-two poems, *Marabou* really is a slim volume, yet American-born Jane Yeh's vivid leaps of imagination make this a first collection to remember. Her topics are eclectic: when Vesuvius erupted, priests' sandals were "soft/Brown mouths, open and dumb as those / Of oxen", while, in a contemporary setting, "When your letter comes, dogs will bark / Up and down the street. The tomatoes in the garden / Will explode like fireworks" ('Correspondence'). Her spectrum of voices includes those of ghostly Cumbrian sheep, a piece of china, a royal painting and a seventeen year old "teen spy".

Marabou ranges widely from the superb 'Double Wedding, 1615', spoken by Anne of Austria and Isabella of Bourbon on the day their single lives were ceremoniously stifled and their pearls "fitted just the length / To choke us", to the reminiscences of the bird playing the part of Harry Potter's Snowy White Owl on film, who confides: "Between takes, I did leg-lifts in my trailer". There are a few syntactical oddities towards the end of 'The Pre-Raphaelites' but mostly her deft use of language is invigorating, thought-provoking, and like a breath of fresh air.

Over eighty poets are represented in Valentina Polukhina and Daniel Weissbort's *Anthology of Contemporary Russian Women Poets*. Their translators include poets Maura Dooley, Ruth Fainlight, Elaine Feinstein, Carol Rumens, and Derek Walcott. The generous poetry selection is followed by a review of contemporary women artists and poets by Elena Fanailova, a piece by Dmitry Kuzmin on young women writers, biographies, and a valuable bibliography that includes anthologies, websites, and periodicals as well as the poets' individual works.

There is something other-worldly about many of these poems – not just because they sometimes open like Olesia Nikolaeva's "You can go on holiday now, you can dabble in verse" or Tatyana Shcherbina's "They cut off my hot water" – lines which remind Western readers how life is very different in Russia – and not even because they often contain more allusions to the 'soul' than is usual. What struck me most was how easily heavily metaphorical or cryptic poems co-exist and share kinship with the many that are more readily accessible, like Vera Pavlova's, "This is the way a row of official tulips / commands you 'Do not pick the flowers', / hoping that they'll be picked up when it gets dark". Several of these poets, like Irina Ratushinskaya (whose evocative 'Thus you lived your life without regret' is here), left Russia many years ago. Others, like Polina Barskova, whose admirable 'Evening at Tsarskoe Selo' wittily celebrates the great Anna Akhmatova, went to live abroad more recently. Many, like Stella Morotskaya, remain in their homeland. There is pain and suffering, but also humour and wit in this collection. Morotskaya's 'Tomato', from her 'Erotic Fruit' cycle, provides the latter: "Tomato is so vulgar and lustful… with its own brutal, greedy kiss, / when it is being turned completely inside out, / and it's unclear who is sucking whom". From the taste of a poet's last breath (Barskova) to a mother's conversation with her embryo (Linor Goralik), there is more here than Russia.

Robyn Bolam's anthology, *Eliza's Babes: four centuries of women's poetry in English*, c.1500-1900, was published by Bloodaxe in November 2005.

Ecstasy, Torture

WILL STONE

Inna Lisnianskaya, *Far from Sodom*, trans. by Daniel Weissbort,
Introduction by Elaine Feinstein, Arc Visible Poets 14, £8.95, ISBN 1904614140;
Michael Hofmann, ed. *The Faber Book of 20th Century German Poems*,
Faber, £9.99, ISBN 0571197035

"Isn't it though the Russian way / to torture oneself ecstatically, / to laugh bitterly, to weep sweetly / and to dance upon a straw?" asks Inna Lisnianskaya in a poem entitled 'I don't consider myself one of the fortunate'. After reading this collection of her poems taken from the last three decades, one can surely only reply in the affirmative. Arc has provided an English readership with one of the leading Russian women poets of the modern era, sensitively translated by Daniel Weissbort.

Lisnianskaya, born in Baku in 1928 of Jewish descent, has been writing for some forty years; but her work was suppressed during the Soviet years and only now has she enjoyed a renaissance as one of Russia's foremost poets. Lisnianskaya however eschews self promotion, preferring to slip back into an area of shadow where only the poem is left visible:

> Reminiscences are for those who selflessly seek
> Traces of self in mortality.
> Memory is what is imperceptible,
> As its water content is to the body.

As Elaine Feinstein and Weissbort concede, any Russian woman poet must inevitably run the gauntlet between those high priestesses Akhmatova and Tsvetaeva; but, whether Lisnianskaya shows evidence of a 'conversational tone' reminiscent of the former or the vibrant strains of her lexical music can be traced in some measure to the latter, she is altogether an original voice, her spare writing showing great precision in highlighting their own uneasy correspondence with time and death. Fortunately, this voice is safe in Weissbort's hands. He manages, through finely-tuned employment of assonance and rhyme, to produce English versions which seem altogether comfortable in themselves. Take the poem 'Instantaneous' from 2002, for example:

> The arrow of the instantaneous sun

Has pierced me to the core.
What is, is; as for what was –
Only the shadow of a wing, an oar.

Any superfluous knowledge for me is
Like fluff from under the gate.
The wind pleases me
And alien is rumour's breath.

Only the wind brings happiness,
Like the smell of freshly baked bread.
The wind does not know what has happened,
And is not dismayed by what's ahead.

Lisnianskaya is at all times concerned with the existential trials of awareness, but manages to harness or flush them out through everyday events, unglamorous subjects, simple observations of nature; whilst at the same time imbuing her poems with a passion and charged honesty.

"The man who laughs has simply not yet had the terrible news" writes Bertolt Brecht in his famous poem 'To those born later'. Such a well-aimed 'spear', one of many launched and as ever morbidly enhanced by the black humour on its tip, would seem to encapsulate the general mood of existential resignation in the face of that incontrovertible despair which dominates German poetry in the twentieth. And the leading speaker at this convention of competing darknesses? Brecht of course, whose poetry marches well here in a variety of versions by different translators. Brecht is thrillingly accessible, even passed through the sieve of English translation. He is inevitably labelled political, but it's the resilient humanity and stoicism in the face of a growing awareness that all firm structures have collapsed, which for me articulates the force of his poems. Brecht's expertise, in making nonsense of senselessness with the least possible padding and rhetoric, has been handed down to successive generations of German writers with variable results. But nobody does it better than the master. Furthermore, his poems have an eerie resonance for our own time. Take this from the poem 1940, translated by Sammy McLean:

The designers sit
Hunched in the drawing offices:
One wrong figure, and the enemy's cities
Will remain undestroyed.

Though much of the poetry in this volume deals rather obliquely with the catastrophe of Germany in the twentieth century, the poetry of Nelly Sachs is explicit as regards her experience of the holocaust itself. In 'Chorus of the Rescued' she hauntingly portrays the dire prospects for a death camp survivor:

> We the rescued
> From whose hollow bones death had begun to whittle his flutes,
> And on whose sinews he had already stroked his bow –
> Our bodies continue to lament
> With their mutilated music.
>
> We, the rescued,
> Beg you:
> Show us your sun, but gradually.
> Lead us from star to star, step by step.
> Be gentle when you teach us to live again.

It is tempting, though probably perilous, to see two strands evolving in twentieth century German poetry. On the one hand, there are poets who react to the absurd realities of the world they inhabit in a more familiar and recognisable, dare I say accessible, way. I am thinking of poets like Benn, Grass, Brecht, Enzensberger, Grünbein. On the other there are the more uncompromising, subjective, lyric poets, visionary mavericks who mostly perished in or before World War I, like Heym, Trakl and to some extent the later Peter Huchel. These travel between landscapes both real and imaginary. Heym, in the years immediately before World War I, painted recognisable cityscapes in poems like 'The Demons of the Cities' and 'Umbrae Vitae'; but imbued them with nightmarish visions of decay and insanity. "Through night great hordes of suicides are hurled," affirms Heym with gusto. Unlike the spare poetry of later generations of poets who create unsettling, often razor-sharp, domestic miniatures in the face of external chaos, Heym and certain of his Expressionist contemporaries have poems brimful of morbid imagery and lyrical excess.

However there is much coherence in this anthology too. The masterly 'Dead Girl in the Water' by Heym, for example, sits comfortably alongside 'Little Aster' and 'Lovely Childhood' by Gottfried Benn. With the possible exception of Celan, Trakl is probably the most original and indefinable poet represented here, having retreated behind a visionary language. His haunting, unclassifiable poetry had a powerful influence on Celan but also on Rilke, both of whom are naturally included here. However, Rilke's inward earnestness seems somewhat abandoned amongst these pared down post-holocaust voices: like a well-meaning priest solemnly practicing a sermon in the vestry, unaware that the roof of the nave has caved in.

Later poets in the collection are rather uneven: the poet who stands out for me here is not Durs Grünbein, who seems to have been allocated far too much space, but the wonderfully-named Haücke Hückstadt:

> Back on the train
> The rain thrashed against the windows.
> Drops teared against the edge and hung trembling.
> I took out my book which began with a man's dream
> Of slicing off his prick and burying it.

Though the largely-ignored Tate anthology of *German Expressionist Poetry* (2003) offers a more in-depth treatment of the poets of that generation and also includes original artwork from the period, Hofmann's anthology fills a gap left by the loss to print of Michael Hamburger's immense bilingual collection of the 1970s. Although mysteriously omitting a number of significant figures, such as Erich Fried and Ilse Aichinger, the collection is a solid attempt to reconstruct in the English language one of the main pillars of European poetry. Anyone who doubts that poetry can sustain the human spirit after the annihilation of practically everything else should read this book.

Will Stone's new translation, *To the Silenced – Selected Poems of Georg Trakl* was published by Arc in November 2005.

Bread and Roses

Poetry Review this Spring includes writing from the US and Ireland as well as the best new poetry from Britain. Piotr Sommer sends a *Letter from Warsaw* and Yang Lian speculates on the inner space of poetry. Elsewhere, Daniel Weissbort reviews Ted Hughes's writing for children while Helen Farish reassesses Sharon Olds.

Poetry Review 96:1 – out April 2006. Available in all good bookshops and at www.poetrysociety.org.uk

ENDPAPERS

...In the fields there were a lot of those clock-winding-up birds (now very rare in Western Europe), those mostly-marching birds in the high grasses called, in Latin, *Crex crex.*
—Tõnu Õnnepalu

Greetings from Estonia!

MIDSUMMER:
POSTCARDS FROM ESTONIA

TÕNU ÕNNEPALU

3 June, on the island of Hiumaa

During the last two days I have twice been advised that I am, in fact, a hare. Hares aren't afraid of me any more. Yesterday there was a big hare on the very cap. I know these hares of the cap. In winter they're white and, if there's no snow, clearly visible. But they run away. Always. This one looked at me with his or her big dark brilliant eye; we were very close to each other, a few metres apart. Only when I moved towards him did he jump slowly away. The fur was also dark brown. Strange that one animal can be so different in summer from what it is in winter. And me? I too have my summer feeling, alert and restless. So, I'm a hare too. Today this became clear: another hare, smaller but not a baby, was in my flowerbed (I never saw a hare in my garden before). He was just there, in the middle of the rainy afternoon. And not too eager to run away either. Looked back, as if inviting me to follow. To the hares' world, my world.

Tomorrow I'll have a garden party. I cut the last big piece of this winter's lamb into chunks and put them in a marinade. Erkki and Anne will come; also Ly from Tallinn. We'll grill the meat. When I was last in Bordeaux I was given two more bottles of good wine. Today, I made a soup from the bones of the lamb; adding some radishes (they're fat and abundant now) and a lot of green things. A workaday meal.

Little starlings (who are no smaller than the big ones) are learning to fly and be independent. No warmth yet. Longing for.

5 June, Hiumaa

The garden party was nice: the first real one, cooking and eating outdoors, this spring. During the day it rained heavily and I was prepared to do it inside, cook in the fireplace. But then in the evening the sky cleared up, it was quite warm and very vivid suddenly. A beautiful evening. All kinds of green. (Valdu's big ash tree is only now coming in to leaf.) First we had a sauna. Erkki brought wine. Ly couldn't come in the end, the trip here by bus is truly long (five and half hours). The lamb was good. I put vinegar, onion, garlic, herbes de Provence, Tandoori masala, salt, sugar, water (and perhaps something else I've forgotten) into the marinade. It's a very special feeling, this grilling meat in the open air. Ancient, prehistoric, a cave man feeling. This smell of burning flesh in the fresh early summer breeze.

My baby hare hasn't shown up today. In a way that's good. If it really means to come to live here, I think it'll soon discover the best leaves are those of salad, carrots and so on.

8 June, manor-house monastery in Esna

Went on a beautiful bicycle tour through Järva-Jaani (St. John, but Järva is the name of the county) and other places. How perfumed nature is now, how generous the evening. The towns ands villages all smell of lilacs. The young needles of spruce have a very fine smell. (Now the nightingale's singing in the park, directly into my window.) I brought white lilacs into my room, but I'll move them to the kitchen later, they smell too strong at night.

I also went to Paide, the county town (twenty kilometres away) and bought a pillow and a lamp. I biked on the old little railway track. It's very nice and somehow mysterious, between the huge spruce; like a tunnel of leaves and grasses. In the spring, in Bordeaux, I biked the old railway tracks (*pistes cyclables* now) and didn't know that this summer I'd do the same thing here. I didn't even know that these routes (and old stations) exist here. In the fields there were a lot of those clock-winding-up birds (now very rare in Western Europe), those mostly-marching birds in the high grasses called, in Latin, *Crex crex*. I like their loud voices (crex! crex!): it's like winding up not a clock but eternity. The eternity of a young summer night

Now I have more letters to write. The mysterious night light burns there in the sky, here in my window.

10 June, Esna

Last night I was too tired for writing. Today was so full of physical work that it's made me somehow excited. And the fine rosy new moon is in the luminous summer night-sky. A remote nightingale still singing. The cuckoo just finished.

Today we started the garden seriously. *We* means mostly a village boy with a very modern New Holland excavator. What he did would have been almost impossible (I mean, I'm not patient enough) to do by hand. In old manorial times yes; with docile, strong peasants and serfs. But now, with our impatient egos: no. So the tractor excavated a lot of huge rocks and bricks. The bricks once formed an ingenious greenhouse heating system. It was a huge, high greenhouse, rather a winter garden, an orangerie. Now its high limestone wall is like another Roman ruin, and will protect the garden from North winds and late frosts. Also it will reflect and store the day's sun.

There are a lot of springs here. A little cold and limpid river runs out from the earth. The manor was built near of these springs. Its water is good and pure.

The meadows are smelling so strongly, sweetly and bitterly in the night. And Hiiumaa I hardly remember now. As if it were a previous life, cold and windy.

Look at the beautiful moon.

30 June, Esna

Yes, awake: eyes wide open, like a hare, really. But I'd like to sleep, too, a bit more. Still, it is not so bad at all. Rather a wonder. Summer's starting its highest blossoming. Meadows are spearing their perfume over the roads. With whom or what I've fallen in love, if I have, I don't know. Just admiring, adoring the way the things are.

8 July, Hiumaa

Imagine how wild my garden here in Kalana had grown during my only-one-month's absence! But that month was June, the month of growth. Now it looks good again; and I'm leaving it again. Yesterday I used my brand new summer-house for the first and last time (the doctor's family will be happy with it, I hope, especially the two young daughters for whom it could be a dream house, a puppet house, their very own secret place) for working on my big *Selected*, which will take poems from the beginning, twenty-two years ago, up to this spring. I liked being there, at that moment. The door was open, young swifts were playing around the little house, I loved my old poems for the first in a long time.

So, so...

Born in 1962, Tõnu Õnnepalu has published four collections of poetry. *Frontier State* (1993), a debut novel published under the literary pseudonym Emil Tode, was a critical sensation and published in more than a dozen languages. Since then he has published a further three novels and *Exercises*, an intellectual diary. He lives in rural north-central Estonia.

LETTERS TO THE EDITOR

What a pleasure to read such a thoughtful and extended piece of poetry analysis in *PR* (Sean O'Brien's 'Rilke and the Contemporary Reader', *PR* 95:3). O'Brien's inspiring polemic on the need for our contemporaries to follow the Rilkean lead of honing technique, extending imaginative reach and commitment to the poetic long run is timely.

Of course, the *Duino Elegies* themselves provide a pretty thorough critique of unsatisfactory artistic performance. The Fifth presents a combined portrait of a troupe of acrobats Rilke knew in Paris and a group from a painting by Picasso. Out of their mix of thumping effort, small craft and aspiring activity comes "only a joyless false fruit". The audience are not so much entertained – so the poet more fondly recalls the acrobats in earlier days when they "were not *able*". These first fumbling efforts have been suddenly "translated" to the "slick Too-much" and Rilke's implication is that a degree of artistry may become a futile end in itself. He concludes with the dismal prospect of Madame Lamort's highly skilled but ultimately moribund art, "dyed with no eye for truth, / but to daub the cheap winter hats of fate". (I quote here from my own translation of the *Elegies*).

MARTYN CRUCEFIX, LONDON

To consider Rilke's appeal largely in terms of the contemporary literary scene gives a very limiting impression of his importance. For it's not only contemporary writers and poets scrutinising his linguistic means for containing the ineffable but publications like 'Rilke for the Stressed Out' (more serious than it sounds) and 'Rilke in the Corporate World' not to mention films and detective stories that bear witness to his powerful appeal to the modern soul. Rilke's appeal, now as then, is rooted in his address to the dilemmas intrinsic to human consciousness itself – as intrinsic at his turn of the century as at ours: alienation from the rest of nature, self-consciousness, inadequate capacity for transcendence, modes of seeing and knowing that categorise, instrumentalise and commodify the world thus disenchanting it, and the loss of soul these processes bring about. His work was a search for a poetic space where the modern soul could dwell – a kind of 'apprenticeship in evolutionary consciousness' in which a poet, with his very particular resources, might be guide. [...] 'Contemporary' in this context implies a short-time-span-ism to whch critic/writers are often susceptible.

JUDY GAHAGAN, LONDON

… AND A SURPRISE RESPONSE

Reading the latest *Poetry Review* because Sean O'Brien's essay spoke to his own interest in Rilke, composer Michael Maxwell Steer found himself setting Lawrence's Sail's poem from that issue…

Sensed

w. Lawrence Sail
m. Michael Maxwell Steer

28 October, 2005

PR Jukebox

Poetry Review Jukebox is a chance to replay high points from the journal's past. Requests, for material from issues published before 1995, are welcomed.

In this musical quarter, the Jukebox responds to a reader's request. Eamon Cooke writes:

> *Poetry Review* has always been an important part of my life since I first encountered it around 1963, with its simple cover incorporating a diagonal white seam. The poems were a revelation as the Editor, John Smith, pointed out that they should be. Even the names of the poets were, to me, new and exciting: Edward Brash, John Fairfax etc [...] I would like to add that magazines like *Poetry Review*, John Silkin's *Stand* and Norman Hidden's *Workshop New Poetry* nurtured my love of poetry over the years and I was, naturally, very pleased to have my own collection published in 2002.

Eamon Cooke's nominations included Gavin Bantock's "fine long poem 'Ichor' (*PR* Winter 1966/7)", from which we print extracts:

Gavin Bantock
sections from Ichor

My mouth is wide open,
my teeth are stopped with mercury and silver,
my tongue is a strand of seaweed
hung-up outside the shore-house to tell the weather,
and the fisherman's oracle says, No rain.

No rain in the valley of fluttering books.
Only the derelictions of war
and gusts of amputated wind
and motionless birds.

*

I am lying on my face
with coral in my mouth, and macaroons in my hands,
and rope-soled shoes on my feet with gravel in them,
sand in my eyes, and the smell of burnt sugar in my nostrils,
and a geometrical compass stuck in my navel.

*

I have not been honest with word.

*

We were going down a long stairway somewhere in South Europe;
or maybe in a North Welsh valley on a wet day, down the Roman Steps.
I can't remember where it was we were going down.

We took in deep breaths, and smoked in the open air,
and talked of Arab boys and sheep-bells.
I can't remember any sound conclusions.

Except that we were going down somewhere.

*

The world is full of stories I have heard before,
and legends that are beautiful survive,
and sometimes I have told them to myself
to hear the slow reiterations echo round:
the sound is beautiful to hear, of ancient stories,
the sound is beautiful to hear, and I have heard
my fill of stories moving in the world
and legends that are beautiful survive.

Editorial

The National Poetry Archive, a sound archive of poets – living and dead – reading their own work, has just opened its web-pages for business (www.poetryarchive.org/). As well as substantial recordings (contemporary poets read for up to an hour) there are lesson plans, access notes and biographies. At its launch, at the British Library, Andrew Motion spoke about the importance of retaining the "sound-sense" as well as the "page-sense" of a poem; and this musical grammar, the importance of its aural-spatial logic, was demonstrated, through the Library's impressive sound-system, by Edith Sitwell (recorded) and Seamus Heaney (live).

Perhaps "The Music of It" is a tautological title for an issue of a poetry journal. At any rate, there's some degree of redundancy: if poetry isn't only music, it's difficult nevertheless to imagine a poem with no claim to musicality. John Kinsella bears down hard on this kind of claim when he writes, in this issue, on denaturalising the (music of the) line-break. "My poetry is a direct result of my politics and ethics, and form for me is a box to be pushed against," he says. "[…] I don't want my poems to leisure or pleasure […] I want my poems to suggest and to bother – to irritate, and to instigate."

A mistrust of fluency, then, can be a mistrust of ideology; of whatever specific set of cultural values are the poetic "common sense" of a particular language and era. The modernists of the 1920s and 30s understood this when they taught their readers to mistrust the realist project with its God's-eye narrator. Who nowadays can be so sure of their place in the order of things, they asked, that they do not experience themselves reflexively, self-consciously? John Berger reminds us that, even in dispossession, lives which "are mostly grief" are "interrupted by moments of illumination [which] arrive by way of tenderness and love – the consolation of being recognised and needed and embraced for being what one suddenly is."

Poetry Review doesn't pretend to solve the great questions of the social globe, any more than it's in thrall to experimentalism, or what Jean-François Lyotard identifies as the avant-garde's ceaselessly self-revising conscience. But it can keep refreshing the poetic norms. This issue features translations from other languages and eras, each of which must re-create a sound-sense as well as a page-sense for the original; a process subject to local, contemporary tastes yet closer – in musical terms – to interpretation than improvisation.

Some sense of musical inevitability must emerge in the newly-translated poem. Where does this inevitability come from? Is it translator's luck? Or is there something in the deep grammar of language which "comes across" from one version to another? Taking late Hölderlin as his example, Heidegger says, "For, strictly, it is language that speaks. Man first speaks when, and only when, he responds to language by listening to its appeal." It is this listening – to the *semantic music* of language – which the best translation, like the best poetry, achieves.

That most musical poet Michael Donaghy wrote about poetic form as a dance floor, a formal terrain which guides and engages poet and reader into mutuality. We might extend his metaphor into the ante-room in which poet and translator practice for public display. Simon Armitage's poem in memory of Donaghy, which ushers in the group of elegies in this issue of *PR*, was specially written for a celebratory event with which London's South Bank Centre honoured that poet this winter. "The Music of It" is dedicated, therefore, to Michael Donaghy.

FIONA SAMPSON

THE 2005 GEOFFREY DEARMER PRIZE

Poetry Review is pleased to announce that the 2005 Geoffrey Dearmer Prize has been awarded to Andrew Bailey for 'Cave Painting' (*PR* 95:1).

This year's judge, the distinguished poet, literary biographer and translator Elaine Feinstein, said that 'Cave Painting' "seems to realize an imagined past while having a sad resonance for our own age". She also enjoyed Andrew's accompanying poem 'Lodestar, Polestar, i.m. Peter Redgrove'.

Feinstein adjudged Valeria Melchioretto, "a very close contender [...] whose poem ('Finding Myself in a Pair of Fisheyes', *PR* 95:3) is both linguistically ingenious and uneasily disturbing". Melchioretto is Highly Commended.

The annual Geoffrey Dearmer Prize is awarded to a new poet, who has not yet produced a full collection, for work published during the year in *Poetry Review*. The Prize is awarded through the generosity of the Dearmer family to honour the noted World War One poet and Society member. *Poetry Review* is very grateful to the donors and to Elaine Feinstein.

CONTRIBUTORS

Antonella Anedda is one of the most influential Italian poets writing today. Her books include *Nights of Western Peace* (1999, international Eugenio Montale Prize) and *The Catalogue of Joy* (2003, finalist for the Viareggio Prize).

Simon Armitage's latest collection, *Universal Home Doctor* (Faber, 2004) was shortlisted for the T.S.Eliot Prize.

Sarah Arvio is a poet who won the Rome Prize 2004. She is from New York.

John Berger's work across art history, politics, theatre and writing was celebrated in spring 2005 with a London festival, *Here Is Where We Meet*.

Kate Bingham's second collection, *Quicksand Beach*, comes out from Seren in March 2006.

Sarah Corbett's collections are *The Red Wardrobe* (1998) and *The Witch Bag* (2002), both from Seren.

Neil Curry's most recent collection is *The Road to the Gunpowder House*, published by Enitharmon Press.

Arjen Duinker (Delft 1956) has published a novel and nine collections of poetry. His next collection is *And that? Infinite* a collaboration with French poet Karine Martel.

Andrew Elliott was born in 1961. He lives in Glasgow.

Helen Farish's *Intimates* won the 2005 Forward Prize for best first collection.

Antoninette Fawcett is writer-in-residence at the Norman Nicholson project, Millom.

Elaine Feinstein's *Collected Poems and Translations* (2002) was a PBS Special Commendation. Her *Anna of All the Russias* is reviewed on p.92.

Tamara Fulcher lives in Peeblesshire. She is working towards her first collection, *Yellow*.

Choman Hardi, born in Kurdistan, moved to the UK in 1993. Her first collection of poetry in English, *Life for Us*, was published by Bloodaxe in 2004.

W.N.Herbert's *The Bumper Book of Troy* and his co-edited anthology, *Strong Words: Modern Poets on Modern Poetry*, both appeared in 2002.

John Kinsella's latest books include *The New Arcadia* (WW Norton, 2005), *America* (Arc, 2005) and *Doppler Effect: Collected Experimental Poems* (Salt, 2004).

Inna Lisnianskaya, born 1928, is one of the most admired contemporary Russian poets. Unpublished for many years in the Soviet Union, she has received both the State Prize of Russia and the Solzhenitsyn Prize. Her *Far From Sodom*, also translated by Weissbort, is reviewed on page 108.

Herbert Lomas's tenth collecton is *The Vale of Todmorden* (Arc, 2003). He is a Knight of the Order of the White Rose for services to Finnish literature.

Sarah Maguire is the Founder Director of the Poetry Translation Centre at SOAS.

Her books include three collections of poetry and the anthology, *Flora Poetica*.

E.A.Markham's *A Rough Climate* (Anvil Press) was shortlisted for the T.S.Eliot Prize in 2002.

Michael Maxwell Steer's song-cycle *Sonnets to Orpheus*, settings of 12 of his own paraphrases of Rilke's *Sonnets*, was recently recorded by Francis M Lynch and the Argonaut Ensemble and tours festivals in 2006. http://msteer.co.uk/

Chris McCabe's first collection, *The Hutton Inquiry*, was published by Salt in 2005.

David McDuff's translations include Pia Tafdrup's *Queen's Gate* (Bloodaxe 2001) and, forthcoming with Stina Katchdourian, Tua Forsstrom's *Selected Poems* (Bloodaxe, 2006).

David Morley's review of W. S. Graham and John Heath-Stubbs appears on page 102.

Dennis O'Driscoll's *New and Selected Poems* was published in 2004. His *Exemplary Damages* was Seamus Heaney's 2002 Book of the Year.

Amir Or's latest collection in *English is Poem* (Dedalus, 2004). Published in twenty-three languages, his awards include the Prime Minister's, Bernstein and Holon Prizes.

Michael Ossei was born in South London in 1978 and works in Camberwell.

Mario Petrucci's 'Trombone' was written during a recent residency at BBC Radio 3.

Estill Pollock's most recent collections include *Fields and Standing Waves* (Flarestack, 2004) and the *Blackwater Quartet* cycle (Kittiwake Editions, 2005).

Peter Porter's latest of more than twenty collections is *Afterburner* (Picador, 2004).

Chris Preddle's pamphlet collection is *Bonobos* (Biscuit, 2001).

Tony Roberts has published two collections: *Flowers of the Hudson Bay* (Peterloo Poets) and *Sitters* (Arc).

Robin Robertson's third collection, *Swithering*, is the Poetry Book Society Choice for Spring 2006.

Lawrence Sail's poems set to music include the sequences *Six Songs and Out of Silence*, both collaborations with the composer Isabelle Ryder included in *The World Returning* (Bloodaxe, 2002).

Will Stone's review of Michael Hofmann and Inna Lisnianskaya appears on page 108.

Pia Tafdrup, who has published eighteen collections of poetry and been translated into 21 languages, won the Nordic Council of Literature Award in 1999 and was made a Knight of the Order of Dannebrug in 2002. These poems are from *The Whales in Paris* (Gyldendal, 2002).

Daniel Weissbort edited *Modern Poetry in Translation* for some 40 years. He has published numerous translations, mostly of Russian poetry, edited anthologies and published a number of collections of his own poetry.

CODA:

101 Differences Between Poetry And Popular Music

after Tom Leonard

CHRIS MCCABE

Nobody queues up all night to get tickets for a poetry reading.

I don't remember carving the names of my favourite poets into a desk at school.

No one shouted "Judas" when Geoffrey Hill dropped the end-rhymes from his poems.

I can't recall the last time I had a drawn-out discussion about the concept of a poetry book.

The greatest praise you can give to a lyricist is that their work is "pure poetry".

The greatest praise you can give to a poet is that their work aspires towards the tonal qualities of music.

If T.S. Eliot had said that he was bigger than Jesus this would have had more to do with an inflated sense of the self than actual sales of *The Waste Land*.

The song happens only when it is played, the poem sits patiently and waits ("You're frozen, when your heart's not open").

The emotional aspect of poetry is in that life is continually passing in all the time you don't visit the poem. With music, your life sits squat as the song joyrides past: if you miss a description of its face, it's gone for good ("past the leisure centre, left at the lights").

Music acts as a mnemonic for the moment. Poetry forgets the details of its genesis, hence the Lost Quotations board.

If you want to read something that justifies the speed, energy, violence, contradictions and innovations of popular music then you read the prose of Paul Morley. If you want to read something that justifies the speed, energy, violence, contradictions and innovations of contemporary poetry then you read the prose of Andrew Duncan. Paul Morley appears on *Newsnight Review*, Andrew Duncan doesn't.

For the question, "how far can music go & still be called music", you could assemble a party of willing explorers to set out on the road of discovery. Although the outcome of this would be similar for poetry, you would have to walk that road alone.

When rolling a narcotic cigarette on a vinyl sleeve it is impossible not to comment on the association between the artistic quality of that sleeve and the drug experience itself (*Dark Side of the Moon*; *Electric Ladyland* etc.). In Amsterdam, as you were preparing to roll, I handed you Robert Creeley's *Later* and you said "great, a hardback".

A record that skips is similar to being interrupted time after time on the same line of poetry

A record that skips is similar

The Poetry Society presents

Under The Influence

A Reading Series in association with the *London Review of Books*

16 March 2006	**John Hartley Williams** under the influence of Shelley
18 May 2006	**U A Fanthorpe** under the influence of Browning
20 July 2006	**Peter Porter** under the influence of Matthew Arnold and Arthur Hugh Clough
21 Sept 2006	**Helen Dunmore** under the influence of Keats
23 Nov 2006	**Ruth Padel** under the influence of Tennyson

All events held at London Review Bookshop, 14 Bury Place, London at 7pm. Nearest tube: Holborn
Ticket prices: £10 (£5 LRB subscribers and Poetry Society members)
Season ticket for all five events: £45 (£20 LRB subscribers and Poetry Society members) Bookings: 020 7420 9896

THE POETRY SOCIETY